Atari Projects:
50 Fun Projects for Your 8-Bit Home Computer

Atari Projects:
50 Fun Projects for Your 8-Bit Home Computer

Jason H. Moore, Ph.D.

Scitari Computing Press
2019

I would like to thank my family for their loving support. I would also like to thank Mr. Bill Lange for his critical reading of the book prior to publication.

First Printing: 2019

ISBN 978-0-578-55642-0

Scitari Computing Press
P.O. Box 530
Wayne, PA 19087

www.atariprojects.org

Contents

Introduction

I grew up Atari in the 1970s and 1980s with an Atari 2600 followed by a 400 and 800. I was fortunate to have the foresight to hang onto my Atari 8-bit computer stuff and acquired my father's collection as well. I started collecting Atari hardware in the early 2000s when it was plentiful and cheap. Between 2000 and 2004 I amassed a substantial collection from thrift stores and flea markets in the Nashville area. When I moved, it all got boxed up, where it stayed until just recently. I have had tremendous fun the last few years unboxing and using my Atari collection.

As I got back into the hobby, I had to relearn how to make use of it all. I also learned about many new hardware and software options such as SIO2PC for connecting the Atari to a modern computer. As expected, much of the information about old and new Atari computing was spread across multiple books and websites with sometimes limited documentation. As I learned how to complete projects, I decided to document them so others like me could more readily find what they needed. Further, as a busy professional, I often don't have time for long projects. I decided to focus mostly on projects that could be completed in less than an hour. This led to the website at atariprojects.org. This book is an edited version of some of the projects listed there. I have tried to present each of the 50 projects in a logical sequence that would allow someone new to the hobby to progress from purchasing hardware, learning how to use it, exploring software, programming, and learning about useful resources.

I hope you find the website and this book helpful for making the most out of your Atari 8-bit computing hobby. The Atari story is an amazing one, and there is no question that the Atari 400 and 800 were ahead of their time when they were released. Display list interrupts, redefined character sets, and player-missile graphics enabled by the ANTIC and GTIA chips were innovations that allowed Atari to dominate graphics and animation in the late 1970s and early 1980s. We are fortunate to be able to relive that history now as much of the hardware and software are still available for collection and use. Jump in, have fun, and keep the excitement of Atari alive for future generations!

1. Purchase an Atari Computer (1-2 Hours)

Prerequisites. All you need for this project is a web browser if you plan to buy from an online auction site and about $100 to $300 of cash. Expect to spend about one to two hours researching and choosing a system to buy.

Introduction. If you are reading this book it is very likely that you already have one or more Atari 8-bit computers. However, if you don't own an Atari, and would like to, I have a few tips here for how to get started. My favorite is the Atari 800 that was released along with the 400 in 1979. My first computer was a 400 that my family purchased in June of 1982 at the Famous-Barr department store outside St. Louis, Missouri for $399. The 400 was originally designed by Atari to be a video game system replacement for the popular 2600. They ended up including a cumbersome flat membrane keyboard that was needed for some popular games. We upgraded to an Atari 800 with more memory and a standard keyboard a little over a year later. I personally think the design of both computers is awesome. I have an 800 on my desk now that is my go-to machine. I still have my original 800 from childhood and have picked up two more recently. However, I don't recommend the 800 as a first Atari computer for several reasons. First, most only have 48K of RAM and thus won't be able to load some of the later games and software that require 64K. Second, they are rarer and tend to be more expensive. Also, it can be hard to find one in good condition. I recommend the Atari 800XL as a first 8-bit computer. This one comes with 64K of RAM and there are a ton out there for purchase. They also have nicer keyboards than the later 65XE and 130XE models. I personally like the top-loading cartridge slot on the 800XL. Cartridges are harder to insert on the 65XE and 130XE. The 800XL has a smaller desk footprint than the 800 as well. You can pair this with an Atari 1050 disk drive that has the same case design and colors (see photo below). I don't recommend getting the 1010 cassette drive. These are notoriously flaky due to aging drive belts that are difficult to replace. Cassettes are also a real pain since they take so long to load and often don't take on the first try. I also do not recommend buying a printer since there isn't much to do with them now. If you are curious, I recommend the Atari 1020 plotter and/or the 1025 dot matrix printers. I have both and you can still find supplies for them. I will cover these in later chapters. So, an Atari 800XL and 1050 disk drive will get you started for much Atari fun.

Instructions. There are several options for securing an Atari home computer. Where most people start is eBay (http://ebay.com). These days there are usually a dozen or more 800XLs on eBay ranging in price from $50 to $250 or more depending on the condition and what else is included. $100 is a reasonable price to pay for one of these if it is clean and in good condition. Expect to pay $150-$200 if it comes in a box and maybe more if it is new in box (NIB). There are some new ones that show up from time to time, but they are usually expensive. The 1050 disk drive usually sells for $50 to $100 depending on the condition and whether it is boxed. So, you should expect to pay $150-$200 for both the 800XL and the 1050. Be patient. These come up all the time on eBay and you likely will not need to wait too long to find a good deal. I will cover additional purchasing strategies in a later chapter.

eBay is of course not the only game in town. If you are looking to spend less there are other options. First, there are other auction sites you can try including Goodwill (https://www.shopgoodwill.com) and Offer Up (https://offerup.com). You can also find them on Amazon (http://amazon.com). Craigslist (https://craigslist.org) also sometimes has Atari stuff. Some other options are the Atari Age marketplace forum (https://atariage.com/forums/forum/6-buy-sell-and-trade). I also highly recommend the Atari Age Facebook page that is quite active (https://www.facebook.com/groups/atariagemarketplace). Lots of things come up here and they are often cheaper than eBay. The best bet might be to invest the time into finding local hardware. This is covered in the next chapter.

In the early 2000s when I put much of my collection together it was possible to find Atari computers and game systems at thrift stores and flea markets. I used to routinely pick up 8-bit computers for $10-$20. Sadly, those days are long gone, and it is very rare to find Atari stuff locally. The supply is dwindling due to age, and nostalgic collectors with money to burn are buying up what is left. I expect the market will crash at some point, but probably not in the next 10 years.

Comments. My best advice is to be patient. Don't rush into any purchases. The nicest items come from collectors and they will often provide this note in the auction description to let you know it is a quality item that has been cared for. Something to keep in mind is that much of this stuff is brittle with age. Make sure the seller packs it carefully. I recommend a box within a box and lots of bubble wrap. I also recommend sturdy new boxes that won't crush under the weight of other boxes. I have had several items including an 810 disk drive arrive with a cracked case. There are many horror stories about this online. Very frustrating. Happy hunting!

2. Tips for Finding Local Hardware (15-30 Minutes)

Prerequisites. All you need for this project is creativity and persistence. Expect to spend about 15 to 30 minutes coming up with a game plan. The execution will take much longer!

Introduction. The easiest place to find Atari hardware and software is on eBay. However, even the most common Atari goodness is way overpriced. There is also the problem of shipping that can leave your items cracked or worse. The best place to find Atari stuff is through local connections. The prices are better, and you don't have to deal with the uncertainty of shipping. The following are some tips for maximizing your success.

Instructions. My **first tip** is to find local sellers on eBay, Facebook, or similar. Even though buying on eBay is challenging it is sometimes possible to use these sites to identify local sellers that are close to you. For example, eBay provides the location of the item in the listing. Facebook Marketplace allows you to limit a search to a specific radius based on miles. Reach out to the buyers and ask them if they have other Atari items they would be willing to sell. I recently scored a local Atari 1040 ST that was cross-listed on eBay and Craigslist in my city. Interestingly, the seller had it $50 cheaper on Craigslist. I also recently discovered a Facebook page for yard and garage sales in my area.

My **second tip** is to post a wanted ad on Craigslist. Craigslist can be a good way to find local Atari stuff. An even better strategy is to post a wanted ad. Make sure to say that you are a collector and that you will not resell stuff for a profit.

My **third tip** is to post a wanted ad in your local newspaper or community website. My most successful local efforts have come from posting to a local community news and announcements website. These posts cost about $35/week to reach about six local towns. I do this several times per year when I know I have some upcoming time to drive and pick up stuff on a weekend. I have done this four times over the past year and three of these posts have landed fairly large lots including a 400, 800, 800XL, 410, 810, 850, etc. One of the people I picked up from called me back several months later to let me know they had found some additional stuff. This has been very fruitful and the prices I paid were about half what eBay would have been. There are still people that have this stuff in their basements taking up space!

My **fourth tip** is to post flyers at local stores and libraries. I haven't tried this yet, but it is on my list of things to do. I can't imagine this wouldn't yield something and it is free!

My **fifth tip** is word of mouth. Talk to all your local friends and family and let them know what you are looking for. Ask them to ask their friends and co-workers. This hasn't yet paid off for me, but it might for you!

My **sixth tip** is to visit flea markets and community rummage sales. I used to do this back in the early 2000s and that is where I found much of my current collection. I have been to a few flea markets over the last few years with limited success. However, I know other Atari collectors that have had some good scores. If you have the time this might be a fruitful avenue. One strategy would be to talk to sellers and let them know what you are looking for. Even bring pictures! They will then keep an eye out for you. Establish a relationship and check back with them each week or every so often. Give them your contact information.

My **seventh tip** is to join or start a local Atari user group. If you live in a larger town or city there might be an Atari user group you could join. This would be a great way to meet people who usually have stuff they are willing to part with or swap for. If not, start your own Atari group! I am hoping to do this in my city. I think this would be a great source of contacts for Atari hardware and software.

My **eighth tip** is to explore and post in the Atari Age (https://atariage.com/) forums marketplace. Atari Age can be a great place to find Atari stuff and prices that are generally less than what you would find on eBay. This is because the people buying and selling are collectors and enthusiasts and are often more motivated to offer a fair price. I have found local people this way. There is a special thread for want ads and you could make it clear that only local sellers should reply. Be sure you only post in the appropriate Marketplace forums. These kinds of posts are not welcome elsewhere on the forums and users will be quick to let you know that.

My **ninth tip** is to attend a vintage computer festival or other retro-computing event. If you are lucky enough to live within driving distance of a retro computing event such as the Vintage Computing

Festivals (VCF) you might be able to find good hardware and software from attendees who bring extra stuff they want to part with. These events usually set up a room where people can sell stuff. I recently attended the VCF East meeting in Wall, NJ and there were definitely some Atari items there to buy. I ended up buying a book I didn't have.

My **tenth and final tip** is to set up a booth or table at a local festival. Most towns have one or more festivals that are held in the summer or fall. If you are really hardcore you could pay to have an Atari table or booth where you could meet people who might have stuff they are willing to part with. I have never done this and don't know anyone who has so consider this a risky move. Most festivals charge at least $200-$300 for a table like this so it would really need to pay off to make it worth it. Might be a good way to advertise a new Atari user group while also looking for stuff to buy.

Comments. It gets harder and more expensive to find Atari hardware and software these days. The supply is shrinking, and the interest is rising. What this means is that we all need to work harder to get those items that we are looking for. I have had moderate success with a few of the strategies listed above. I plan to try some of the others. I will update the list online as I get feedback and have new success stories to share. Let me know if something has worked for you and I will add it to the list. Happy hunting!

3. Read the Purple Book (2-3 Hours)

Prerequisites. You will need the *Your Atari Computer* book or PDF. Expect to spend about two to three hours reading this book.

Introduction. I recall having two books when we first got our Atari 400 and then 800 back in the day. The first was *Atari BASIC* as a self-

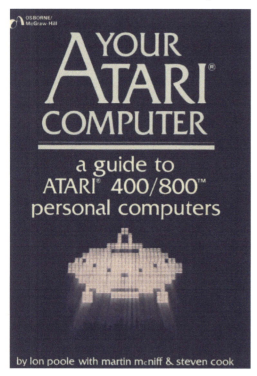

teaching guide (see Chapter 34). The second was *Your Atari Computer* (a.k.a. the purple book) by Lon Poole, Martin McNiff, and Steven Cook, which was published in 1982. I remember devouring the purple book cover to cover. I even typed in the player-missile graphics demo in BASIC, which is shown on the cover. This book is a bible for new Atari computer owners as it goes over the basics of Atari hardware and BASIC programming. It is still relevant for those getting into Atari 8-bit computing for the first time or for the first time since the 1980s. It is fun to read for experienced Atari users as well. I highly recommend it.

Instructions. The purple book is available on The Internet Archive (http://archive.org) in the original edition or the updated edition for the XL line of computers. You can also find plenty of used copies on eBay and other used book sellers. New copies of the XL version are available for $12.95 from Best Electronics (http://www.best-electronics-ca.com/xe_game.htm#soft6).

Comments. A classic! If you own five books about Atari 8-bit computers, this must be one of them. Enjoy!

4. Test the RAM of an Atari Computer (10-15 Minutes)

Prerequisites. If you have an Atari 400 or 800 you will need a *SALT* or similar cartridge or an Atarimax Maxflash or similar flash device to load the ROM. Software for testing RAM is built into the XL and XE series of computers. Expect to spend about 10 to 15 minutes testing the RAM of a single computer.

Introduction. I remember being really interested in the diagnostic tests that were included in the Atari 1200XL. These allowed you to test 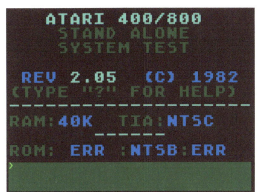 the RAM and other things, such as the video, sound, and keyboard. What a great idea to have this built-in and available on boot up. The diagnostic software was also included in the other XL and XE models. I assume these were moderately useful back in the day, although I don't recall ever finding any bad hardware. These are much more useful now as we acquire old hardware that is often not functioning.

Unfortunately, these diagnostics were not available on the Atari 400 and 800. I have acquired a number of these machines and like to test them as they come into my collection. There are several diagnostic programs available (e.g. *The Monkey Wrench*) although I have only tried the *Stand-Alone System Test* (*SALT*) which I present here. *SALT* came in cartridge form and there is very little information about it online. The ROM from the cartridge is hard to find as well and is not available from common sources such as The Internet Archive.

Instructions. **Step one.** Find and download the *SALT* 2.05 ROM from the Atari Age 8-bit computer forum post titled *Super SALT Diagnostic Carts* from February 28 or 2012 (see post #15). You can also buy a *SALT* cartridge for $25 from Best Electronics (http://www.best-electronics-ca.com/800.htm).

Step two. Load the ROM onto a flash cartridge such as the Atarimax Maxflash (https://www.atarimax.com).

Step three. Boot your Atari 400 or 800 with the flash cartridge or *SALT* cartridge inserted.

Step four. You will see an intro screen with the name of the program and a green dialog box at the bottom.

Step five. Enter a question mark (?) at the prompt and hit return. This will bring up the diagnostics menu.

Step six. Choose the R option and hit return. You will need to choose the number of 8K RAM modules to test. Note that the *SALT* program takes up 8K so you will only be able to test 40K or 5 modules. Hit return to start the RAM test.

Comments. There are a few threads on the Atari Age forums about *SALT*. You might also try some of the other diagnostic programs such as *The Monkey Wrench*. Note that SALT only tests 40K of RAM since the program takes up 8K. You might need to switch the positions of the RAM cards to identify which one is defective.

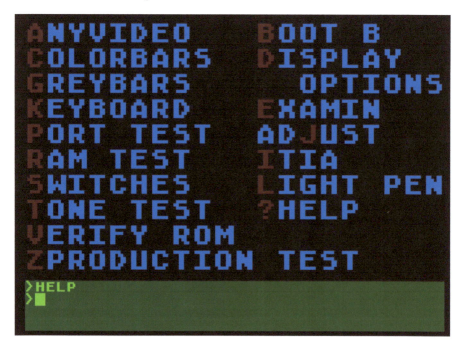

5. Purge Dangerous Power Supplies (15-60 Minutes)

Prerequisites. All you need for this project are some labels and a pen if you want to list the compatible devices on the power supply. Expect to spend about 15 to 60 minutes labeling and gathering power supplies for e-recycling.

Introduction. If you are like me and have many different Atari home computer models and peripherals, then you also have many power supply units (PSUs). As I have been rediscovering my collection I am also learning about the differences between the different PSUs. I certainly didn't appreciate these differences when I was a kid because I only had one computer and several peripherals. It is important to know the differences because the wrong PSU could cause your Atari to malfunction or even shorten its lifespan. Some PSUs can fail and destroy your beloved Atari.

Fortunately, there are some resources on the web that spell all of this out making it easy to figure out what PSUs you have and how they match up to different hardware. A good place to start is the Atari FAQ page (https://mcurrent.name/atari-8-bit/faq.txt) on power requirements for Atari computers (see Subject 6.2). Not only do they explain how the PSUs work, but they list each difference model number and what their specifications are. This is good to spend some time with. There is also a good discussion of PSUs on the Best Electronics website. The website is a bit difficult to navigate but has some useful information. They also sell PSUs. There are a few good threads about this on the Atari Age site, but many of these posts leave out key details for those not in the know. It will take some time to read through all of them.

Instructions. Pull out all your PSUs and attach a small label to each that lists the model numbers (e.g. 400, 410, 800, 810, 800XL, etc.) that the unit is compatible with. Use the FAQ linked above for the necessary information. This might take longer than the 15-60 minutes indicated above depending on how many PSUs you have. Having these labeled will take the guesswork out of finding the right PSU the next time you want to power up a computer or peripheral. It will also help reserve the lifespan of your hardware. A worthy exercise that will save you pain and suffering in the future.

An important note of caution. There is one PSU for the XL/XE series of computers that is known to fail often and, when it does it, runs the risk of taking your computer with it to the great beyond. This particular PSU has model number C061982 and shipped with the

600XL and 800XL. It is compatible with the 600XL, 800XL, 65XE, 130XE, and XEGS. The model in question is black, has a black label, and is heavier than the other PSUs because the unit is filled with epoxy. I had two of these in my collection and have since e-disposed of them. To the top left is a photo I took of one of them. These are sometimes called the "ingot" (i.e. gold ingot) or "boat anchor" because of their size, weight, and utility.

There are several others with this model number that are all ok. There is a large black unit and one that is white that both have vents matching the vent design on the XL series. I have a couple of these, and they are ok to use. There is also one about the size of the ingot above except that has a silver label and a slightly different case design. These are also ok. I have one with the silver label (see photo to bottom left).

Comments. I have a variety of PSUs including some from vendors other than Atari. It was helpful to compare the voltage and amperage of each to know what they are compatible with. The most common PSU I had was the C017945 that is compatible with the 400/800/1200 and 810, 822, 850, 1010, 1020, and 1050. This is a desirable multipurpose PSU.

A good long-term goal would be to find modern replacements. Although this reduces the authenticity of your system, it might be the best bet for protecting the hardware from failure. Regardless, gaining a working knowledge of your PSUs is important.

6. Clean an 810 or 1050 Disk Drive Head (15-30 Minutes)

Prerequisites. For this project, you will need a Phillips-head screwdriver, a Q-tip, and some rubbing alcohol. Expect to spend about 15 to 30 minutes taking apart and reassembling the 810 or 1050.

Introduction. I started out back in the early 80s with an Atari 400 computer and a 410 cassette recorder for storing programs. Working with the 410 was tedious and at times painful. We upgraded the next year to an 800 and an 810 disk drive. What a difference! Being able to save and load programs from a floppy disk was pure heaven compared to cassette technology. I still have my original 800 and 810 and am very fond of the design of both. This is my favorite of the long list of Atari hardware models. In fact, I took my 810 to my high school electronics class, cracked it open, and soldered in "The Chip" from Spartan that allowed copying protected software.

The 810 disk drive is getting harder to find as they age and malfunction. You can find them on eBay for $50 to $250 depending on the condition and whether the original box is included. I purchased two on eBay in 2018 each for less than $100. There are three main issues I have found with 810 drives. First, they are kind of big and have brittle plastic which means they crack easily. My original 810 case cracked in a move. One of the two I got on eBay this year cracked due to poor packaging. Be sure to communicate with the seller to make sure they use extra bubble wrap and an interior sturdy box with packing around that. I have five 810s and three are cracked. Second, some of them are yellowed which means they won't match your 800 computer in color unless it is equally yellowed. I am not a big fan of the yellowing and all my 800s are pretty close to the original tan color so I notice it. There are methods using peroxide chemicals to reverse the yellowing although I haven't tried this yet. Finally, it is likely the 810 drive read/write head needs to be cleaned. This is true from normal use and certainly true after sitting in someone's basement for the last 30 years. I have done this and include below some of the details on how this is done. Some general posts on repair can be found on Atari Age (https://atariage.com). The 810 and 1050 operators and field service manuals from Atari can be found online. Both are easy to clean.

Instructions. Cleaning the drive head is relatively easy. The following steps can be applied to the 1050 drive as well.

The **first step** is to remove the cover. You may first need to remove the small circular tabs on the top of the case that cover the screw holes. Remove the screws with a Phillips-head screwdriver. They are old so proceed gently.

The **second step** is to gently lift the arm that holds the felt pad that presses the disk against the head and clean the head with a Q-tip dipped in alcohol. Note that the felt pad can also wear out creating unreliable contact between the disk and the head.

The **third step** is to reassemble the cover and you are done. I hope your old drive works like a dream!

Comments. There is always that moment when you aren't sure whether it is the drive or the disk that is the problem. I have hundreds of disks and more than 95% seem to have survived and still work (amazing, right?). Be sure and try a few different disks to rule that out as a cause. Disks wear out faster over the years if they aren't protected from the elements. Also, some claim that centering the disk in the sleeve can increase the likelihood of a disk working. I never did this as a kid, and don't know if it is a real thing. My disks that don't work appear to be dead on arrival (DOA) for the rest of time. Something to try though!

7. Upgrade a 1050 Disk Drive with the Happy Board (15-30 Minutes)

Prerequisites. You will need a 1050 disk drive and the Happy enhancement board. Expect to spend about 15 to 30 minutes on the installation.

Introduction. The Atari 810 disk drive could read and write single-density disks with about 90K of data. Atari's follow-up drive was the 1050 that was billed as dual-density. This was false marketing since the drive could only read and write about 130K of data. It was not true double-density. Some refer to the 1050 as providing 'enhanced' density since it was better than what the 810 could provide but less than other true double-density drives such as the Indus GT that could offer about 180K of data storage.

Happy Computing was formed in 1982 to provide special chips that could be installed in the 810 and then 1050 to provide true double-density data storage and faster read and write times. They also allowed you to make copies of commercial disks with copy protection. A drive modified with a Happy board was called a "Happy drive". The good news is you can buy newly made Happy boards and install them in a 1050 drive with no soldering!

Instructions. I purchased my Happy board from 8-Bit Classics (https://www.8bitclassics.com) for $39.99. They ship you the board and floppy disk with the software, although my disk was DOA. You can also purchase these for about the same price from Atarimax (https://www.atarimax.com/). The installation is relatively easy and instructions are provided online. I will not provide all the details here. Basically, this involves removing the cover, removing the metal RF cage, removing two chips, and seating the Happy board in the longer of the two chip slots. There are helpful YouTube videos if you want to see someone go through the installation steps.

A few tips. **First**, I didn't need to unplug all seven cables connecting the drive mechanism to the circuit board as the instructions say. I only needed to remove the one toward the front and could simply tilt the drive backward to remove the circuit board from the case with the other six cables still in place. **Second**, you need to remove the RF cage. Once you have the circuit board out, turn it over with the attached drive mechanism on the bottom. The RF cage has little metal tabs that have been twisted to hold the two cages from both sides of the circuit board together. You either break these off or simply twist them so they fit through the slot. Once you do this you can remove both metal RF cages. I disposed of mine as I don't think they are needed unless you have a radio nearby. **Third**, insert the circuit board as instructed. The

instructions and the videos on YouTube are clear and I didn't have any problems. **Finally**, put it all back together again. Mine worked on the first try and was able to boot disks. You can hear a faster chirping noise on boot.

Comments. I have my Happy board successfully installed but have not yet tried out all the software options. There are also some posts about Happy drives and the related software on Atari Age. You can sometimes find Happy 1050s on eBay if you don't want to take the time to do the install yourself. Eight Bit Fix (https://www.eightbitfix.com/) sells them for $125 and had them in stock at the time of writing.

Since my software disk came dead on arrival, I am making some new ones. I do this by finding the ATR disk image files for the Happy software and booting them from my PC using an SIO2PC cable (see Chapter 13) with the *Atari Peripheral Emulator* (*APE*) software from Atarimax (https://www.atarimax.com) running on the PC. The *Happy Warp Speed Menu* Rev. 7.0 ATR disk image can be found online. This includes everything you need to get started, including their own version of DOS, diagnostic software, a sector copier, etc. Once booted, I can make new 5.25-inch disks on my real drive connected as drive two.

8. Purchase an Indus GT Disk Drive (15-30 Minutes)

Prerequisites. All you need for this project is a web browser or time to find hardware locally. Expect to spend about 15 to 30 minutes on your purchase.

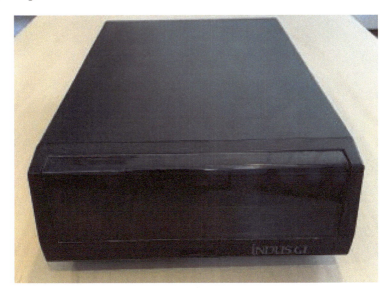

Introduction. My favorite disk drive is the Atari 810. It was my first and I love the aesthetics. However, the 810 could only read and write about 90k of data and was thus considered single-density. The 1050 was an improvement as it could read and write about 130k of 'enhanced-density' data but was not considered double-density because it wasn't the full 180k. You can make a 1050 true double-density by installing the Happy board that also makes it much faster (see Chapter 7). There were several true double-density drives available back in the day. The best of these, and considered by some to be the best overall, is the Indus GT. We had several of these in the 1980s and fortunately I still have them.

The Indus GT is a lovely piece of hardware. As shown in the photo above, it comes in a sleek form factor that is smaller than the 1050. It is also very attractive in all black and with a smoke-colored see-through plastic cover that pops up to reveal the face of the drive. The cover not only looks cool, but it helps keep dust and debris out of the drive case. Included in the front of the drive is an LED display that shows the track and sector the drive is on as it reads and writes. There are four buttons on the front panel as well. The first is labeled Protect that will toggle the write-protect mode. The second is labeled Drive Type that will indicate on the LED the drive number (1-4) that is set with the switches on the back of the drive. The third is labeled Track that will display the current track on the LED. The final button is labeled Error that will display the error code on the LED in the event something has failed.

I highly recommend an Indus GT for your collection and for daily use. I love mine and prefer it to my Happy 1050. Below are some tips for finding one.

Instructions. The Indus GT drives are much harder to find than the 810 or 1050. There were fewer made, and they are in high demand. At the time of this writing there were only four on eBay ranging in price from $75 to $125. In my experience, most tend to sell for at least $100, especially if they include the storage case and original software and instruction manual. I haven't run across any of these in the wild. The three that I have were all mine from the 1980s. Glad I saved them! Unfortunately, eBay may be your best bet unless you know someone personally willing to part with one. Good luck!

Comments. One of the cool things about the Indus GT is that it is driven by a Z80 processor. Some have been able to run the CP/M operating system on the Indus thus turning it into a Z80-based computer. I haven't tried this, but it is on my list of things to do. It seems to require a 64K RAM expansion to make this work.

You can find a PDF of the instruction manual for the Indus GT online as well as other documents.

9. Purchase an 850 Interface Module (15-30 Minutes)

Prerequisites. All you need for this project is a web browser or time to find hardware locally. Expect to spend about 15 to 30 minutes on your purchase.

Introduction. The Atari Serial Input/Ouput System or SIO was designed to allow the computer to communicate with peripherals such as the 810 or 1050 disk drive. An advantage of the SIO is that multiple devices could be chained together. A major design consideration was allowing the Atari computer to communicate with peripherals without the need for installing an internal card. Unfortunately, many devices such as third-party printers used a different communication port called an RS-232. Atari made the 850 Interface Module to allow communication with devices that used the RS-232 port along with devices using the SIO connectors.

These are still somewhat useful today as printers and modems (e.g. modern Wi-Fi modems) often use the RS-232 port. Fortunately, they are relatively easy to come across on eBay and other sources.

Instructions. The 850 Interface Module can be easily found on eBay for around $50 to $75. At the time of writing, there were about six available and most were listed for $50.

Comments. I have seen some criticism of the 850, but I think it has been a useful device to have. I still have mine from childhood and acquired a second as part of a lot I picked up locally. My only beef with the 850 is the design. I would have been thrilled if the 850 could have sat sandwiched between my 810 disk drive and my 820 printer with the same form factor. Unfortunately, the footprint of the 850 is smaller than the 810 which means it needs to sit on your desk somewhere. I find this awkward. Also, it is very lightweight which means it doesn't stay where you put it. Another design question is why Atari didn't release one in the style of the XL and then XE series? The Atari FAQ (https://mcurrent.name/atari-8-bit/faq.txt) has a lot of information about this peripheral (see Section 6.1.1).

10. Replace the Ribbon and Paper in an 820 Printer (10-15 Minutes)

Prerequisites. All you need for this project is an 820 printer and a web browser for purchasing the supplies. Expect to spend about 10-15 minutes on the purchase and installation.

Introduction. I never had an Atari 820 printer back in the day but always wanted one because it beautifully matches the same style and color of the Atari 800 and 810 disk drive which is my preferred setup that I keep on my desk and use regularly. I recently picked up a lovely 820 for about $150 on eBay. It arrived in great condition with very little yellowing (see photo above). So happy to have this! I have been shopping eBay daily for more than a year to find this gem. Thanks to the seller for getting it to me in one piece.

Now that I have an 820 my next step was to find paper and ribbon for it. Fortunately, Best Electronics (http://www.best-electronics-ca.com/) has both paper rolls and ink ribbons in stock. Unfortunately, you can only buy one at a time. I assume their stock is limited and dwindling fast. I paid $8 for the ribbon and $6 for the paper roll. Not

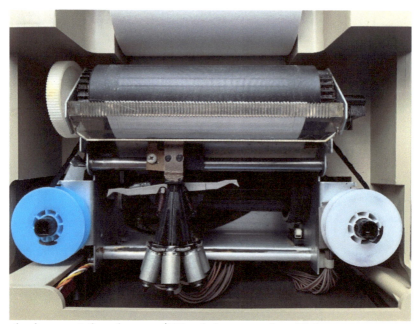

too bad except they have a $50 minimum order. This means you must purchase more stuff from them. I picked up a shrink-wrapped *Moon Patrol* cartridge which I didn't have. However, you might not want to pay that much just to get ribbon and paper.

Given the limitations of Best, I decided to look around to see if I could find the ribbon and paper elsewhere. I also posted on an Atari Age thread about this. This turned out to be a lot harder than I imagined. I am still searching for paper (more on that later) but I did manage to track down ribbons. I found a company called Ribbons Unlimited (https://www.ribbonsunlimited.com/) that sells all kinds of old ribbons for retro printers. If you go to their Dot Matrix page there is a list of old printer makers that includes Atari. If you click on Atari, they list ribbons for a few models including the 1025. However, the 820 was not listed. So, I emailed them what I was looking for and they were responsive and said they would investigate it. Bingo! After a few days they emailed me with a new listing for Atari 820 5/16" black ribbons! They sell them for $8.50 each which is just $0.50 more than Best, and you can order as many as you want. Problem solved. A photo of the part number is below.

I have not yet found a good source of paper other than Best. I will post an update online if I track down paper rolls. The problem is that much of what is available in the ~ 4" width size is thermal paper. I am holding out for regular paper. I suppose thermal paper would work, but I don't really want the chemicals.

Instructions. **Step one.** Purchase a paper roll from Best Electronics for $6. Email them and indicate you want Atari 820 40 Column Printer Paper roll (CB101922). You will need to add to the list to make it at least $50. You can pay with Paypal.

Step two. For the ribbon I recommend the one from Ribbons Unlimited. You can pay online with a credit card and order as many as you want. They are $8.50 each (part #6N085).

Step three. Follow the instructions in the official Atari 820 Operators Manual that you can find online.

Comments. Finding supplies for these old machines is getting more difficult by the day. I had to work hard to find these ribbons. I should probably order a few more and stock up. Who knows when these will disappear for good! Let me know if you have a good source of paper rolls. Still looking...

11. Replace the Ribbon and Paper in a 1025 Printer (10-15 Minutes)

Prerequisites. All you need for this project is a 1025 printer and a web browser for purchasing the supplies. Expect to spend about 10-15 minutes on the purchase and installation.

Introduction. I never had an Atari printer in the 1980s. We had an Epson MX-80 dot matrix that worked quite well. So, I have been slowly

acquiring and trying all the Atari printers I can get my hands on. My first was a 1020 that had to have the plastic gears replaced. This is covered in the next chapter (12). Next was an 820 printer that I had to track down ribbons and paper for. This was covered in the previous chapter (10). I have it hooked up to my 800 and 810. I have two 1027 printers that will be the focus of future posts to the Atari Projects website. They also have part issues. I do not yet have an 822 thermal printer. The focus of this chapter is the 1025 that I recently acquired.

From what I can tell, the 1025 dot matrix printer was the workhorse of the Atari printer line. These were very common back in the day and thus are relatively easy to find on eBay and through other sources today. I recently picked one up on eBay for about $90. It is in really good condition with very minor signs of wear which is why I was willing to pay so much for it. There are five on eBay at the moment and are priced around $50 to $75. My first impression as I was taking it out of the box is how insanely heavy these things are. I had no idea. The 1025 weighs in at more than 13 pounds! A solid beast of a printer. Because of the weight it doesn't move or shimmy while printing. It just sits there like a rock doing its thing.

I have been very impressed with the quality of the print from this machine. Below is a floppy disk directory I printed from *Atariwriter*. The left is a photo of the disk directory on my Sakata CRT monitor. The middle is the 1025 print. The right is from the 820. The 1025 is much sharper than the 820 (as expected). From what I can recall about my Epson, the 1025 seems like it has a better print and seems fairly quiet. I am impressed so far. Below are some instructions for finding ribbons and paper for this lovely printer.

CRT		1025		820	
BOTLSND.BAS	003	BOTLSND.BAS	003	BOTLSND.BAS	003
DOS.SYS	039	DOS.SYS	039	DOS.SYS	039
DUP.SYS	042	DUP.SYS	042	DUP.SYS	042
E.C	012	E.C	012	E.C	012
HAMRSND.BAS	002	HAMRSND.BAS	002	HAMRSND.BAS	002
JETSND.BAS	003	JETSND.BAS	003	JETSND.BAS	003
MADMAG.BAS	069	MADMAG.BAS	069	MADMAG.BAS	069
PHONESND.BAS	003	PHONESND.BAS	003	PHONESND.BAS	003
PUMPKIN.BAS	018	PUMPKIN.BAS	018	PUMPKIN.BAS	018
SIRENSND.BAS	003	SIRENSND.BAS	003	SIRENSND.BAS	003
513 FREE SECTORS		513 FREE SECTORS		513 FREE SECTORS	

Instructions. The **first step** is to order ribbons from Ribbons Unlimited (https://www.ribbonsunlimited.com). They have a great product with solid personal service. The ribbons are $8.95 each (part #1930ATA). My understanding is that this type of ribbon is pretty standard and fits many typewriters. You can probably find these lots of places. For example, these are available from Amazon for $10.50 (https://www.amazon.com/gp/product/B0136W6OS0/ref=ppx_yo_dt_b_asin_title_o03_s00).

The **second step** is to order paper from eBay. I got my tractor fed dot matrix paper for about $10 per 100 sheets. The prices vary a bit depending on the supplier but are generally in that range. I chose eBay because I could find smaller quantities. You can order from places like OfficeMax, but they tend to come in larger quantities (e.g. 1000 pages). Note that you can also use single sheets of modern printer paper.

The **third step** is to install the ribbon and paper. If you need help installing the ribbon and paper, you can consult the 1025 manual that can be found online. The instructions are clear, and it is not hard to do. There is even a little diagram inside the printer for how to thread the ribbon.

Comments. I didn't think I would like the 1025 printer this much. It is really awesome and a nice addition to my collection. Note that I had to connect this through a 1050 to work with my 800. It did not work running the SIO cable through my 810 drive. This makes sense but is good to confirm.

---

12. Repair a 1020 Printer (30-60 Minutes)

Prerequisites. For this project, you will need a 1020 plotter printer, ink pens, a roll of paper, and a set of 3D-printed gears that are needed to replace the stock gears that are usually broken. This fix will take you about 30 to 60 minutes.

Introduction. I had an Epson dot matrix printer with my original Atari 800. It served me well but wasn't that great with graphics and was

only black and white. I recall drooling over the ads for color printers in *Compute!* and other magazines but never got the chance to try them. So, I jumped at the chance to purchase a new in box (NIB) Atari 1020 plotter printer from an online seller for $35. I finally got a chance to open this beauty up and give it a spin.

I knew from reading online that many 1020s don't work because of a cracked plastic gear that helps move the paper up and down. Without a functioning gear the plotter is unable to make accurate vertical lines. Fortunately, you can purchase 3D-printed replacement gears online from a printing service called Shapeways (https://www.shapeways.com/). Search for the Alps X/Y Plotter Gear. They currently sell them for $12 for a set of three. There are videos on YouTube and discussion threads on Atari Age (http://atariage.com) on how to fix these printers. There is also an official Atari service manual for the 1020 online although I didn't find this all that useful. The service manual does say not to remove the pen cassette with the pens in it. I did this several times before reading this and hope I didn't damage something. They repeat it twice with one time in bold, so I guess it is important!

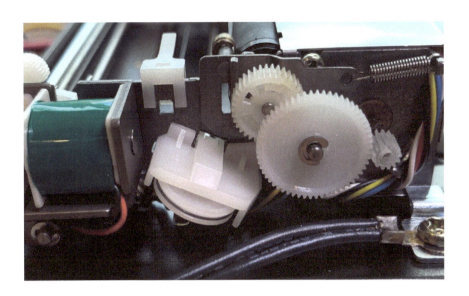

Instructions. The **first step** is to remove the top cover and the front panel. First, remove the dark plastic piece on top that covers the roll of paper. Turn the printer over and remove the two rubber feet on the front. The two on the back don't need to be removed and are glued on. This will reveal two screws. Remove these screws and the three others that are recessed. You will need a Phillips screwdriver for this. Then

turn the printer over so it is right side up. The top white piece is connected to the black front piece by some plastic clasps. What I do is gently lift the back part of the white top piece. You will notice that it is connected to the black piece. At the same time slide both forward. Be gentle because the back piece is also connected to the main circuit board by some wires that are connected to the 1020 buttons. Once detached, you should be able to tip both pieces up and away from unit thus exposing the innards of the system.

The **second step** is to replace the gears. The photo above shows the right-side gear assembly. There are three gears there that help control paper movement. The tiny one on the right is the one that needs to be replaced. Simply slide it off with your nail and slide on the replacement gear. The photo above shows my cracked gear.

The **third step** is to reassemble the case. The case goes back the same way you took it off. Make sure the tabs on the bottom of the black front piece stay parallel to the table and slide in below the circuit board. These tabs are where the screws below the rubber feet go to hold this part of the case on. It should all click into place easily. Screw in the five screws and you are done.

Comments. To test my plotter, I typed in a BASIC program that is included in the 1020 manual that comes with the unit. You can find this online. The one I selected plots sine waves in blue, green, and red and then plots the axes in black.

Note that you can get new pens and paper from Best Electronics (http://www.best-electronics-ca.com). The pens of course are hit or miss and dry out easily. You can see that in my plot below. The red is weak.

There is also an *Antic* magazine article from February of 1986 (Volume 4, Number 10) about mastering the 1020. There are some sample BASIC programs included.

You might also check out *Renderific* from Kevin Savetz (https://github.com/savetz/Renderific). This is an SVG renderer that draws images on the 1020.

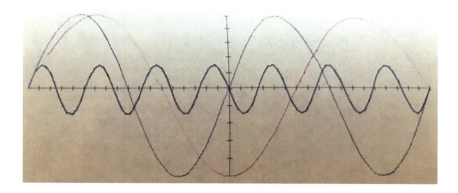

13. Connect Your Atari to a PC (15-30 Minutes)

Prerequisites. All you need for this project is an SIO2PC circuit board with an SIO cable to the Atari and a USB cable to the PC. Expect to spend about 15 to 30 minutes on the purchase and installation.

Introduction. Cartridges and floppy disks are great but sooner or later you will want to tap into the huge archive of software that is available on the internet. You can certainly boot these with an emulator such as *Altirra* (see Chapter 27). However, there is nothing like running software or playing games on original hardware. Fortunately, modern hardware and software makes it easy to connect your Atari 8-bit computer to your PC or Mac to boot games directly from your hard drive. These devices essentially make your Atari think it is booting directly from a disk drive.

My first SIO2PC device I built myself back in the early 2000s. They are much more sophisticated now. One came pre-installed as a mod to an Atari 65XE that I purchased on eBay. The previous owner installed a Cypress USB-UART adapter kit in the 65XE with a small hole cut out of the side of the case for the USB cable. This converts the USB signal to the Atari serial input-output or SIO port. I was happy to get this 65XE for $175 on eBay. I just had to install the Cypress driver on my PC and I was off and running booting disk images from my hard drive using the *AspeQT* software. Unfortunately, this mod didn't work with the *Atari Peripheral Emulator* (*APE*) software from Atarimax that, like *AspeQT*, allows you to boot disk images. The main reason I wanted to use *APE* is that it can serve as a virtual modem allowing you to telnet from your Atari 8-bit computer to a BBS on the internet. I didn't use BBSs back in the day and was really looking forward to exploring these online resources today. This led me to purchase an SIO2PC unit (see photo above) from Atarimax (https://www.atarimax.com/) that is compatible with the *APE* software. I provide instructions below for getting connected to your PC using the SIO2PC and *APE*.

Instructions. The **first step** is to purchase an SIO2PC device from Atarimax. The USB version is $69.95. I got the one with dual SIO ports. These were backordered when I purchased mine in September of 2018 and it took about three weeks to come in.

The **second step** is to install the SIO2PC driver. This comes on a CD-ROM that is distributed with the device.

The **third step** is to install the *APE* software. Note that the software comes with a cripple delay that lasts about 20-30 seconds. You need to register the software to get rid of this. I am not sure why they cripple the software after you just paid them $69.95 for the hardware.

The **fourth step** is to run the *APE* software and then click on the Start APE Now button.

The **fifth step** is to connect your Atari to the SIO2PC with an SIO cable. Connect the SIO2PC to your computer with a USB cable. You should see a message at the bottom of the *APE* software that says "APE USB interface detected and configured" if all goes well.

The **sixth step** is to download an ATR file and load it into *APE*. You can find many great ATR files on the Atarimania website (http://www.atarimania.com), for example. Once you have downloaded an ATR file, load it into *APE* by clicking the load button (i.e. the file folder icon). This places it into virtual disk drive one.

The **seventh step** is to boot your Atari. If all is working, it should start beeping and load the file. That is it!

Comments. A fun thing to do is to copy images loaded this way to real disks. This is covered in a later chapter (26). A downside of Atarimax is that their web page isn't very good. I found it difficult to navigate and some of the document links are broken.

I would also love to have a case for my SIO2PC since it comes as a bare circuit board. Some have 3D-printed cases for these. None of these seem to be for sale.

14. Purchase an Atarimax Maxflash Cartridge
(30-60 Minutes)

Prerequisites. You will need an *Atarimax Maxflash Cartridge*, *USB Cartridge Programmer*, A to A USB Cable, and *Maxflash Studio* software. Expect to spend about 30 to 60 minutes on the purchase and setup.

Introduction. I love the ease of use of cartridges compared to cassette or disk. Fortunately, there are some easy modern ways to get software ROMs from your PC onto a cartridge for play on original hardware using flash-based technology. I purchased an 8MB flash cartridge from Atarimax that allows me to load up multiple ROMs from my PC and then run them on my Atari 8-bit computers with selection from a nice menu. I recommend this product, although customer support is sometimes lacking.

Instructions. The **first step** is to purchase both the *Maxflash* 8MB cartridge AND the *Maxflash USB Cartridge Programmer Kit*. These are sold separately. The flash cartridge is sold for $39.99 while the programmer kit is sold for $59.99. Together these are not cheap and will set you back about $100 plus shipping. You can purchase both the *Maxflash* cartridge and the programmer from the Atarimax web page (https://www.atarimax.com/flashcart). I think it is a good investment if you love to play games and run software on original hardware. You might not want to spend this kind of money if you are more of an emulator person who rarely breaks out the Atari.

For the **second step**, install the *Maxflash Cartridge Studio* software that ships with the programmer kit. Mine came on a CD-ROM. Run the software.

The **third step** is to plug in the programmer cartridge with the A to A USB cable that ships with the programmer kit. You should see a message in the blue box at the bottom that the programmer is connected.

The **fourth step** is to download ROMs (e.g. .BIN or .ROM files) and drag and drop the ones you want on your cartridge into the free slots of the software. It should automatically recognize them. See a screenshot at the end of this chapter.

The **fifth step** is to plug your *Maxflash* cartridge into the programmer with both labels up. Then press the Synchronize Cartridge button on the bottom right part of the software. The software will start programming your flash cartridge. The process of flashing the cartridge is slower than you think. I have 33 ROMs on mine and those took about 10 mins to flash.

For the **sixth step**, disconnect and run on your Atari. Enjoy!

Comments. This process is easy. I found it much easier than the MyIDE-II that is also sold by Atarimax. An advantage of the MyIDE-II is that it comes with a removable flash card and has some advanced capabilities.

There is also a 1MB cartridge that they sell for $24.99 if you are trying save a few dollars. This will easily hold 50 or more ROMs.

There are many different threads that mention the Maxflash cartridges on Atari Age (http://atariage.com). I won't list them here because there are too many and I couldn't find one or two with primary information. I suggest doing a search in the Atari 8-bit forum and exploring yourself. This might be useful if you encounter a problem or technical question.

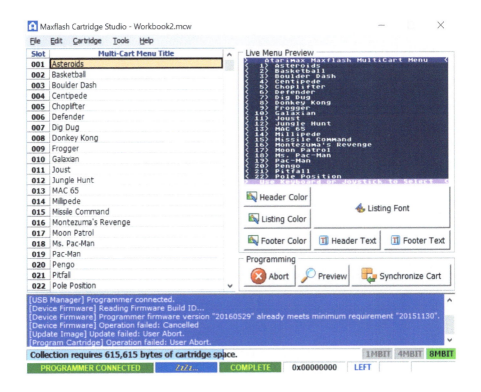

15. Purchase an SDrive-Max Disk Drive Emulator (15-30 Minutes)

Prerequisites. For this project, you will need an SDrive-MAX and microSD card. Expect to spend about 15 to 30 minutes on the purchase and setup.

Introduction. The ability to boot software from SD card devices makes using Atari computers a breeze. These devices allow you to load up lots of executables and ATR files on an SD card and then choose the one you want to use from a menu. One such device that makes this

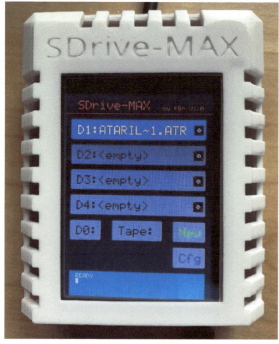 possible is the SDrive-Max that plugs into the Atari via the SIO port, thus emulating a floppy disk drive. I purchased one recently and have been very impressed.

The unit comes with a 16GB microSD card that you can plug into your PC to load files. Once your files are loaded, you plug it into the SDrive and then power it on. One of the cool features of the SDrive is that is comes with a nice touch screen that allows you to load files from a menu into different drive slots. Alternatively, you can boot the Atari from drive 0 which loads a menu on your computer that you can use to select files in the different drive slots. This multiple drive feature would allow you to easily use software that required multiple disks or disk sides. The device also comes in a nice 3D-printed case that roughly matches the style of the Atari XL series with the slanted vents on the sides. It is just a bit bigger than an Atari 800 cartridge and a bit smaller than an Atari 2600 cartridge.

Instructions. **Step one** is to purchase an SDrive-Max from the Vintage Computer Center (https://www.vintagecomputercenter.com). These are made in limited batches so they may not be available when you are ready to order one. At the time of writing there were units available in white and grey colors for $95.99. They are also available from The Brewing Academy (https://thebrewingacademy.com/) for $74.95.

Step two is to load ATR files onto your microSD card. There are several good sources of ATR files including Atarimania (http://www.atarimania.com/) and the Internet Archive (https://archive.org/).

Step three is to plug in the microSD card and power on the SDrive-Max unit. Once on, use the menu to select the ATR file in the first drive.

Step four is to plug the SDrive-Max unit into the Atari via SIO and then boot the Atari.

Comments. This is a nice option for emulating a floppy drive and can be used to boot ATR and CAS files. However, these are not mass-produced and are thus in limited supply. Also, I found the documentation to be lacking. Regardless, the device is easy to use and very intuitive, so the documentation isn't really needed. It is also a little pricey at over $100 with shipping. I am very happy I got one and recently purchased a second that work as part of a chain of SIO devices.

There are several Atari Age threads about the device. Here is the original source of the SDrive-Max in German (http://www.kbrnet.de). You can even make your own! Nir Dary has a great tutorial about the device on YouTube. Steve Boswell has a nice webpage about it as well (https://atari8bit.net/everything-sdrive-max).

16. Connect Your Atari to an LCD Screen (30-60 Minutes)

Prerequisites. For this project, you will need an LCD monitor and a composite to S-Video connector. Expect to spend about 30 to 60 minutes on the purchase and setup.

Introduction. I love my Sakata SC-100 CRT monitor that I use with my 8-bit machines. I still have the same one I used back in the day with my Atari 800. As much as I love this monitor, I know it won't last forever. There will come a day when I need to find an alternative. I have started planning for that eventuality by getting what I need to connect my Atari computers to a modern monitor or TV. There are many different options to explore in this space. I will focus here on one of these and save the others for future posts online.

First a bit of background about Atari 8-bit computer video. All of the Atari 8-bit computers have a monitor port that outputs a composite video signal. This is a single-channel analog video signal that is connected to a monitor or TV through a yellow connector that is often found as part of an RCA connector that also includes red and white audio connectors for stereo sound. The single channel of video is called composite because it creates a linear combination of the luminance (luma) that carries the brightness of the video along with the chrominance (chroma) that carries the color. This is super easy and allows you to connect any Atari 8-bit computer with the composite out to a TV or monitor with the composite (yellow) in. Many monitors and TVs from the 1990s and early 2000s have composite in and are still relatively easy to find.

Although the composite signal is easy, you can get much better-quality video by keeping the luma and chroma signals separate and feeding the two-channel signal to an S-Video connector. As I will show below in the instructions, these connectors for your Atari are readily available. To see the difference in quality, I have included below screenshots of composite on a CRT monitor (my Sakata SC-100), composite on an LCD monitor, and S-Video on an LCD monitor. Note the remarkably better quality of the S-Video image. All three of these were taken under the same lighting conditions at the same time. The LCD monitor is a Dell 2001FP 20-inch monitor that was very popular in the early 2000s. The video ports for this monitor are also shown below.

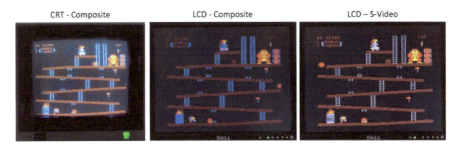

| CRT - Composite | LCD - Composite | LCD – S-Video |

S-Video is clearly the way to go. Unfortunately, only the Atari 800, 65XE, and 130XE provide both the luma and chroma signals needed by S-Video. This is a problem since most Atari 8-bit enthusiasts use an 800XL that only includes the luma signal. The chroma capability is there, it was just never connected to the monitor port in the 600XL, 800XL, and 1200XL. There are instructions online for how to make the connection to enable S-Video on the XL line of computers. There are also Atari Age (http://atariage.com) threads on this that are easy to find.

The final issue is sound. Most LCD monitors don't have sound capability. This means you need to connect the red and white RCA connectors to some speakers. I had a really hard time finding small speakers for the desktop that accepted RCA sound input. Fortunately, there is a Y connector that converts the RCA sound to a 3.5 mm audio connector found on most speakers. Details below in the instructions.

Instructions. The **first step** is to purchase a Dell 2001FP LCD monitor or similar. These can be readily found on eBay (https://www.ebay.com/) for about $50 to $100. You might be able to find them locally for much cheaper since there are still plenty around.

The **second step** is to purchase a composite to S-Video connector. I bought mine from 8-Bit Classics (https://www.8bitclassics.com). Expect to pay about $10 to $25 for one. The photo below shows the

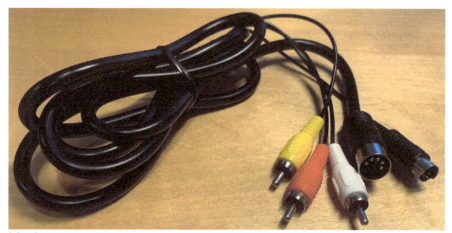

black composite connector that goes to the Atari with the S-Video connector that goes to the LCD screen to the right.

The **third step** is to purchase an RCA audio to 3.5 mm audio

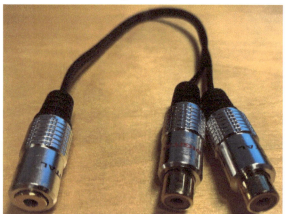

converter. The one I bought I found on Amazon for about $10 (see photo to left).

Comments. I have found getting Atari video onto modern monitors and TVs to be one of the more confusing topics. This is partly because the resources on Atari Age and other sources are inconsistent and often assume the reader has more knowledge about the technical side of video than they probably do. What I described above is relatively easy and S-Video is awesome if you have a 400/800 or XE system.

17. Connect Your Atari to an LED Screen (30-60 Minutes)

Prerequisites. For this project, you will need an LED monitor and a composite or S-Video to HDMI connector. Expect to spend about 30 to 60 minutes on the purchase and setup.

Introduction. In the previous chapter I covered details on how to connect your Atari computer to an LCD screen using composite video or composite converted to S-video. What if you want to connect your Atari to an LED screen using HDMI? Converting composite to HDMI is not as straightforward as converting to S-video because HDMI is a more complex signal. To do a good job of this you really need a professional video processor unit that can cost $500 to $1000 or more. I have not been willing to drop this kind of cash on a video converter solution. There are a number of low-cost converters out there, but you really get what you pay for. I tried three different models and report here on my mixed experience.

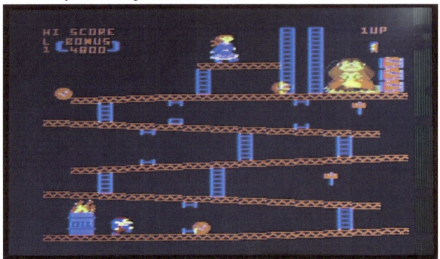

The first one I tried was the Armor3 that was recommended by several different people on Atari Age and elsewhere. This one comes in a small plastic case with composite video and sound in and HDMI out. It runs about $20 and is widely available. Above is a screenshot I took of an Atari 130XE running *Donkey Kong* with the HDMI out connected to a Dell 43" LED monitor. This was not as bright as the one below and always comes with the green stripes on the right side.

The second one I tried was the Neoteck that was also recommended by several different people on Atari Age and elsewhere. This one comes in a small metal case with composite video and sound in and HDMI out. It runs about $20 and is also widely available. Here is the comparable screenshot. This one was a little bit brighter and a tad crisper. It did not have the green artifacts of the Armor3. I like this one a bit better.

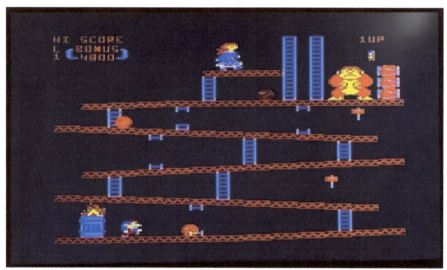

The third one I tried was the Tendak that converts both composite and S-Video to HDMI. This one comes in a larger metal case and runs about $30. I was particularly excited to try this one since the S-video is such better quality than composite. However, my video signal out showed up only in black and white. I tried all sorts of different cables and several different monitors and TVs. No dice. There are a number of negative reviews online that report the same thing. It appears to be a common defect. I have been unwilling to risk another $30 for one of these or another one that converts S-video. Maybe down the road when I get up the nerve to splurge on a more expensive professional video processor.

Instructions. I recommend you purchase the Neoteck to convert composite to HDMI. It worked well for me and the price is right at about $15 to $20. It is pictured in the photo below.

Comments. It is really hit or miss with these cheaper converters. You might need to try two or three as I did to find one that works with your gear. I personally find this one of the more frustrating aspects of retro-computing. For now, I don't plan to spend any more money on this effort.

18. Connect Your Atari to the Internet (15-30 Minutes)

Prerequisites. For this project, you will need an SIO2PC device. Expect to spend about 15 to 30 minutes on the setup.

Introduction. Although the internet was invented before Atari 8-bit computers were released in 1979, it was not available to most of us until years later. I don't recall using the internet until I was in graduate school at the University of Michigan in the early 1990s. I believe I sent my first email around 1993. The only way to connect with the outside world with Atari-bit computers was by using a modem to dial up a Bulletin Board System (BBS) using your phone line. This was both slow and expensive if you didn't have a local BBS to call. Remember how expensive long-distance calls were? I didn't have a modem in the early 1980s and thus had no experience using my Atari "online".

The BBS had its start in the late 1970s and the services were very popular through the 1980s and into the 1990s. If you are interested in learning more, I recommend you watch the *BBS Documentary* that is publicly available (http://www.bbsdocumentary.com/). Very interesting stuff. The sysop war stories are somewhat shocking. A common use for the BBS was to download both public domain and pirated software. There were also early message boards. I show in this post how to connect your Atari computer to a BBS using the Atarimax SIO2PC and *APE* software to allow telnet over the internet to establish a connection.

Instructions. The **first step** is to connect your Atari to your PC using the SIO2PC from Atarimax (see Chapter 13).

The **second step** is to launch the *Atari Peripheral Emulator* (*APE*) software from Atarimax (https://www.atarimax.com/) and load the *850 Express!* 1.1 ATR file. You can download this from the Internet Archive, for example. This is the communications software from the 1980s that we will use on the Atari. I tried several others, including later versions of *850 Express!*, *MPP*, and *BobTerm*. The latter seemed to work best for this task.

The **third step** is to boot the *850 Express!* software from your Atari. If you get a DOS menu simply binary load (L) the filename. Mine was called EXPRS850.COM. A photo of the interface is shown below.

For **step four**, press A to toggle ATASCII mode from the 850 Express 1.1. menu. Also press B to increase the BAUD rate from 300 to something faster, like 2400 or 9600. This is the modem speed in bits per second.

For **step five**, press SHIFT + ! to enter the terminal mode. The terminal should say Connected! with a cursor below it. You are now ready to connect to a BBS using the OPEN ADDRESS PORT command. Here are several to try:

OPEN BROADWAY1.LOREXDDNS.NET 23
OPEN BASEMENTBBS.DDNS.NET 9000
OPEN DARKFORCE-BBS.DYNDNS.ORG 520

The text on the screen should say Trying... and then Connected... After it says Connected, hit RETURN four times. The BBS will then prompt you with some questions. That is it! You are on the internet and connected remotely to a BBS.

Comments. It took me a few hours to figure this all out and I am certainly not yet a BBS expert. There are not good instructions online and many of the Atari Age posts are old and lacking important details. Hopefully my experience trying this will save you some time. Here is a list of other BBS sites you can try with their online status noted (http://www.sfhqbbs.org/ataribbslist.php). Many of these are simple and don't seem to have much content. Many also don't seem to be live. Note that these tend to ask for your personal information including name, address, email, and phone number. This is usually required if you want to create a full account to access more stuff. Nonetheless, they do provide a glimpse into what connecting by phone to a BBS was like in the 1980s. It is fun that these are being resurrected.

It is also worth noting that you can connect your Atari to an 850 interface via SIO and then connect the 850 to a Lantronix or another device via RS-232. Some have used the Lantronix UDS-10 device. From their web page it looks like you need to contact them for a price. You can search the Atari Age 8-bit computer forums for Lantronix to pick up the discussion threads on this. Another approach is to purchase a Wi-Fi modem. I have not tried these options myself and don't know all the details about how to make them work. Projects for another day!

19. Fun with the Atari Touch Tablet (15-30 Minutes)

Prerequisites. For this project, you will need the Atari Touch Tablet and the *AtariArtist* cartridge or software. Expect to spend at least 15 to 30 minutes trying this out.

Introduction. I got an Atari Touch Tablet along with the *AtariArtist* cartridge for Christmas back in the early 1980s. This was one of my favorite Atari gifts ever. I had so much fun with this thing. I really liked making digital art on the Atari 800 and the Touch Tablet made it so easy. The *AtariArtist* software had a great graphical menu that you could use to select colors and drawing modes. You could then click the red button on the stylus to switch to the drawing screen and back again to the menu. This was all very seamless. I still have my original Touch Tablet and picked up another one locally in an original box last year. These are relatively easy to get if you don't have one. You can usually find them on eBay for about $50 loose or maybe $100 if boxed. You can also get them new in the box for $50 from Best Electronics (http://www.best-electronics-ca.com).

A neat thing about these is that they are easy to program for. The X and Y coordinates are mapped onto PADDLE(0) and PADDLE(1) while the left and right buttons are mapped onto PTRIG(0) and PTRIG(1). There is a red button on the stylus that is mapped onto STICK(0). This makes it easy to read the input from the device and use that however you want. I have found two demos that highlight this in BASIC. The first is a simple program that reads the inputs and prints them on the screen. This code appeared in the reader feedback section of *Compute!* magazine from 1986 (Issue 74, page 10). The second program loads some machine learning code to read the inputs during the vertical blank and then turns them into music. I found this one in the book *Atari Assembly Language Programmer's Guide* by Moose and Lorenz (see page 278). You can find the text files and an ATR file on the Atari Projects website (http://atariprojects.org).

Instructions. **Step one.** Purchase an Atari Touch Tablet for $50 from Best Electronics or find one on eBay.

Step two. Try the Touch Tablet with the included *AtariArtist* cartridge. If you got your tablet without the cartridge you can get the

ROM online for use with a flash cartridge like Atarimax. There is also an ATR file for this online. The manual is available online as well.

Step three. Try the two Touch Tablet demos I mentioned above (touchpr.txt & touchmus.txt). You will want to use these on original hardware as the tablet doesn't work with emulators. There is also an ATR file. You can find these files on the Atari Projects website (http://atariprojects.org).

Comments. This was one of the first commercial tablet input devices for any home computer. It was certainly a winner. There is an Alan Alda commercial on YouTube highlighting the device. There is a *Compute!* article from 1984 (Issue 53, page 106) on the tablet and the Atari Light Pen. There is also an Atari Age thread with some great photos of artwork made with the tablet.

20. Tips for Storing Your Atari Hardware (10-15 Minutes)

Prerequisites. For this project, you will need only a web browser. Expect to spend about 10 to 15 minutes on learning some strategies for storing your gear.

Introduction. I got most of my Atari collection in the early 2000s when it was cheap and somewhat plentiful. I could tell as I acquired and cleaned each item that many of the computers and video game consoles were not stored in good conditions. I recall getting a box of stuff that smelled like dog pee. I even found a dead mouse inside an Atari 2600 case. However, since then I like to think I have taken pretty good care of my stuff except for a summer move where it all sat in a moving truck in more than 90°F heat for at least 10 days. The rest of the time my collection has been in air conditioning or climate-controlled storage. I am fortunate that most of my hardware seems to work fine after all these years. The following are some tips for storing and preserving your Atari hardware. Most are common sense while a few take a bit more time. I got this list from a great article in *PC Magazine* (https://www.pcmag.com/feature/355587) that was published in 2017 by Benj Edwards.

Instructions. **The first tip is to remove batteries**. This is an easy and important thing to do. Alkaline batteries corrode over time and can damage the circuitry of your hardware. I purchased an Axlon Andy on eBay in 2018 it came with heavily corroded D batteries. I am saving this cleanup and restoration for a summer project.

The second tip is to keep hardware out of the sun. Almost every Atari computer I have has some degree of yellowing that results from exposure to UV light. In order to minimize yellowing, I keep my computers in the dark when not in use and away from direct sun when on my desk. There is a method for reversing some of this damage called retrobrighting that requires applying something like Salon 40 volume creme that is typically used for lightening hair. I haven't tried this yet but do plan to soon. There are many Atari Age (http//atariage.com) forum threads about this.

The third tip is to replace capacitors. The capacitors on these old systems can fail and leak corrosive chemicals onto your circuitry. I personally haven't had this problem with any of my machines, but it is common enough to worry about. It is easy enough to check under the hood to see if any of your caps are leaking. If so, they should be replaced. This does require some soldering. Some say that leaving the computer on for a few days helps heal the capacitors. I haven't had the nerve to do this, but I do routinely fire up my old machines thinking that using them is better than letting them sit.

The fourth tip is to avoid heat and humidity. This is another obvious one. Storing old equipment in an attic or garage is not a good idea. Moisture and heat are bad for these old machines. As the *PC Magazine* article mentions, mold is very destructive and hard to get rid of. It is better to prevent it in the first place. I have most of my hardware in a basement cabinet in an air-conditioned space that is supplemented with a dehumidifier. If you need one, a dehumidifier can be purchased at a home improvement store for between $100 and $200. Well worth the investment and probably the single most important thing you can do for preservation.

The fifth tip is to keep bugs out. If you are storing your gear in an attic or garage, then bugs and rodents will find their way inside the cases. This has happened to me. Not pleasant and can be hard to clean. The *PC Magazine* article recommends plugging the holes. This is probably a good idea if you must store outside living area.

The sixth tip is to keep an eye on rubber components. I have had several Atari computers with rubber feet that have left chemical marks on the finish of my desk. These degrade over time and some can become liquid making a real mess. Again, best to avoid heat.

The seventh tip is to minimize dust. Dust is another element that wreaks havoc on these old systems. Best to cover in an airtight box if in an open area. I have all my stuff in a closed cabinet.

The eighth tip is to be gentle. I am adding this to the *PC Magazine* list. The plastic on these old machines gets brittle over the years and cracks easily. I lost an 810 drive case in a move due to bumps. I should have packed it better. As you store these items, it would probably be a good idea to avoid stacking them without some cushioning and never put anything heavy on them. I have had several items arrive cracked from eBay shipping including an 810 (see photo on next page). Gentle is good.

Comments. Like I said, much of this is common sense, but a few things like avoiding heat, humidity, direct sun, and dust can go a long way to preserving our beloved Ataris for many years. This general topic was also covered on the *Retro Computing Roundtable* podcast episode 78.

21. Tips for Downsizing Your Collection (10-15 Minutes)

Prerequisites. All you need for this project is willpower. Expect to spend about 10 to 15 minutes reviewing strategies for downsizing.

Introduction. I amassed a pretty big Atari collection back in the early 2000s when hardware and software was easy to come by in flea markets and thrift stores. Looking back, it was a feeding frenzy. I picked up a ton of stuff over about three years. This included consoles such as the 2600, 5200, and 7800 and a wide range of 8-bit computers. For example, I ended up with nearly 20 2600s because they were so plentiful and cheap. I still have all these today and plan to get rid of more than half sometime this next year. I also picked up several other computers including some Commodore, Radio Shack, and Texas Instruments computers.

While it is relatively easy for enthusiasts to find reasons to purchase hardware, it is very difficult to find the willpower to downsize. I certainly struggle with this. My plans to part with hardware are always more ambitious than reality. However, I did recently part with three Atari 5200s. This was hard to do, but the 5200 is my least favorite machine and they take up so much space! My complete list of Atari hardware is on my Atari Age profile (Scitari).

I provide below some tips for how to manage your Atari collection. This of course varies from person to person, but I hope you find a few of my thoughts useful.

Instructions. **My first tip is to identify a finite space.** Perhaps my best decision was to define a finite space where my collection would live. I have a large cabinet in my basement where I keep most of my Atari hardware. My cabinet is about 10 feet long and two feet deep with several bays between three and four feet high. This is where I keep about 90% of my collection. I also have a small closet where I have a few items, a bookcase with software and books, and a desk with the hardware I use on a daily basis. My firm plan is to not outgrow this space. This means that if I want to acquire some new hardware, it has to fit in the cabinet. The 5200s I got rid of freed up almost an entire shelf that could be used for new acquisitions.

My second tip is to get rid of boxes. One of the best decisions I made from a management point of view was to limit my collection of original packaging. Computer and peripheral boxes take up so much space and they are often not in good condition or harbor mold or vermin. I have a few boxes of mostly peripherals and the ones I have tend be small and in excellent condition. I understand the value boxes have to some, but for me it is not worth the space sacrifice. I would much rather have hardware.

My third tip is to decide how many of each you need. I have made the general decision to keep no more than three of each console or 8-bit computer type. For the 2600, my goal is to keep two clean and working units of each type (e.g. heavy sixer, vader, jr., etc.). For the 8-bit computers, my plan for now is to keep three clean and working units of each (400, 800, 800XL, 1200XL, etc.). I am pretty close to this goal with about two to three of each. The only one I have more than three of is the 800XL. I have four of those. The XL and XE series don't really take up much space without the boxes. I can get about eight XL/XE computers on a shelf with each stored vertically (see photo below). This is enough that I can be sure I will have working version for years with replacements or parts in waiting.

My biggest dilemma is what to do with my consoles and computers from other manufacturers. For example, I have a Commodore Vic-20, three C64s, and a 128D along with several peripherals and a bunch of software. I was never a Commodore guy but think it might be fun someday to give these a spin and learn their ins and outs. However, these Commodores and my others take up about 1/4 of my overall space. I very likely will not be able to dive into these other computers until retirement which is still a number of years away. Do I hang onto these and please my future self or get rid of them to free up space for more Atari gear? For now, I have decided to hang onto these since I have a pretty big Atari collection right now and hopefully don't need to acquire much more.

My fourth tip is to remember the joy it brings. Something that has given me some comfort as I part with hardware is the satisfaction that what I am moving out is likely to go to a good home. Often, the people buying on eBay or elsewhere are collectors like us or newbies just getting into the hobby. Either way, someone else will take pleasure in receiving and owning the item.

My fifth tip is to resist the urge to expand now. One of the things that has kept me from impulse buying Atari hardware is knowing that the bottom is going to fall out of the retro-computing market in about 10 years. Most of the people buying hardware are in their 50s or so and nostalgia has hit. This wave of purchasing is likely to wane, thus reducing demand. Also, as people move into retirement there is often a practical need to downsize and simplify. This will create an increase in supply as demand is shrinking. There will of course be less working hardware at that time, but I think the increased supply and decreased demand will outpace hardware failure, thus driving down prices. So, if you are willing to be patient, you may be able to get what you want at much lower prices in about 5-10 years. This will be perfect timing to set up an Atari retirement. That is my prediction, and it has tempered my urge to buy now.

Comments. Coming up with an overall strategy is important for managing what is usually limited space. The urge to own tons of Atari gear needs to be balanced with the reality of life, family, and the burden a large collection will place on whoever has to deal with it when we are gone. Each strategy will be different depending on individual space constraints and preferences (e.g. using vs. collecting). Hopefully the tips above are useful for maximizing the pleasure that comes with Atari.

There was a recent episode of the *Retro Computing Roundtable* (*RCR*) that discussed "uncollecting" (episode #193). There is also an older *RCR* episode that talks about downsizing (episode #90). These can be found online (http://rcrpodcast.com).

22. Explore Disk Operating System Versions (30-60 Minutes)

Prerequisites. For this project, you will need DOS disks or ATR files. Expect to spend about 30 to 60 minutes trying out several different versions.

```
DISK OPERATING SYSTEM II VERSION 2.05
COPYRIGHT 1980 ATARI

A.  DISK DIRECTORY   I.  FORMAT DISK
B.  RUN CARTRIDGE    J.  DUPLICATE DISK
C.  COPY FILE        K.  BINARY SAVE
D.  DELETE FILE(S)   L.  BINARY LOAD
E.  RENAME FILE      M.  RUN AT ADDRESS
F.  LOCK FILE        N.  CREATE MEM.SAV
G.  UNLOCK FILE      O.  DUPLICATE FILE
H.  WRITE DOS FILES




SELECT ITEM OR RETURN FOR MENU
```

Introduction. I vividly remember the excitement of getting my first Atari 810 disk drive and the magic of the disk operating system (DOS). Since we got our 800 and 810 around 1983, the version of DOS I first used was 2.0S for single-density drives. I was of course amazed at the speed of the disk drive compared to the 410 I had used with my 400 for the preceding two years. I had fun learning how to load and save files from BASIC, how to run executables using binary load, how to format disks, how to copy disks, etc. It was satisfying to relearn DOS years later after getting back into the Atari computing hobby.

The first version of *Atari DOS* (1.0) was released in 1979 to coincide with the release of the Atari 400 and 800 and the 810 disk drive. Atari continued to release DOS versions through the XL and XE series of computers. In addition to *Atari DOS*, we used several third-party operating systems including *Smart DOS*, *Sparta DOS*, *Top DOS*, and *My DOS*. Each had their own twist on the basic concept that was represented in *Atari DOS*. These are fun to explore. I have provided a list of some of these below, along with links to the ATR files to each so you can download them and try them in an emulator or burn them to a floppy for use on original hardware.

Instructions. The following is not meant to be a comprehensive list but rather a sampling of the flavors of DOS for the range of Atari 8-bit computers. Check out the Atari DOS Wikipedia page (https://en.wikipedia.org/wiki/Atari_DOS) for more in-depth information about each. Also, these and other DOS ATR files and manuals can be found at Atari Mania (http://www.atarimania.com) and the Internet Archive (https://archive.org).

Atari DOS **1.0** - The first from 1979.

Atari DOS **2.0** - The second version came in single-density (2.0S) and double-density (2.0D) flavors. The 2.0D was briefly released for the 815 dual disk drive that never really made it out into the market and is thus quite rare.

Atari DOS **3.0** - The third version was designed for the 1050 disk drive. Unfortunately, it was not backward compatible with 2.0. This came out in 1983.

Atari DOS **2.5** - The fourth version, released in 1984, that made 3.0 backward compatible.

Atari DOS XE - Released in 1988 for the XF551 drive used with the XE line of computers. Was not compatible with DOS 2.0 and 2.5 or the 400/800 line of computers.

Eclipse Software *TopDOS* - This started out as a mod to Atari DOS 2.0 and grew into a commercial product with lots of interesting features.

ICD *SpartaDOS* - I recall this DOS being very popular in the mid and late 1980s. It was one of the few that had a command line interface.

Optimized Systems Software *OS/A+* - Compatible with Atari DOS 2.0. Also had double-density support. Unique in that it used a command line interface instead of a menu. OSA stood for operating system advanced.

Rana *SmartDOS* - Compatible with Atari DOS 2.0. Also had double-density support.

Comments. I often wonder why Atari didn't build DOS into a ROM and make it available on boot up like they did *Memo Pad* or *BASIC* on the XL series. I assume it was because of memory issues and cost. I guess it also makes sense due to the rapidly changing landscape of disk media and disk drives.

If you are interested in the technical details of *Atari DOS*, I recommend reading the book, *Inside Atari DOS* (1982) by Bill Wilkinson. The text can be found online.

23. Make Floppy Disks (15-30 Minutes)

Prerequisites. For this project, you will need floppy disks, a disk drive, and DOS. Expect to spend about 15 to 30 minutes learning how to do this and trying it out.

Introduction. I am a big fan of cartridges but understand and accept that the floppy disk is important and useful. I still have all my floppies from childhood. I have also accumulated hundreds of floppies from the collections of others over the years. These are really fun to explore, and it is amazing to me that about 95% of them still work. However, there comes a time in your retro-computing hobby when you want to make new floppies for a practical reason or just to relive the experience. Fortunately, you can still purchase new in box floppies from the 1980s on eBay (http://ebay.com). A box of 10 disks sells for about $15. I provide below some simple instructions if it has been a while since you have done this as well. It will all come back quickly!

Instructions. The **first step** is to find a used or new diskette. As I mentioned above, you can find new old stock 5.25" floppies online for about $1 to $2 per disk. You might also find some unused disks in your own collection.

The **second step** is to boot your Atari into DOS. If you already have one or more disks with DOS on it, you are all set and can load it to complete the steps below. However, if you don't have DOS there are several things you can do. First, you can buy used disks with DOS on them from eBay. For example, the Atari Master Diskette that came with different versions of DOS is regularly available on eBay, although there is no guarantee it will still work. Another option is to connect your Atari to your PC/Mac with an SIO2PC cable that then provides access to disk images (i.e. ATR files) through software such as *APE* from AtariMax.

Wikipedia has a nice summary of all the different versions of DOS from Atari and other brands (see Chapter 22). There is an article on "Everything you wanted to know about every DOS" from a 1985 issue of *Antic* magazine (see Volume 4, Number 3). *DOS* 2.5 is a good place to start and will work with all the Atari disk drives. I like *DOS* 2.0S for my 800 and 810 setup. I also used *SmartDOS* back in the day.

The **third step** is to initialize or format the disk. I prefer to use an Atari 800 with an 810 drive, since this is what I used as a kid. This means that I am limited to single-sided (SS) reading and writing and single-density (SD). An SD disk holds about 90K of data organized into 720 sectors of 128 bytes each on one side. You can of course flip the disk over and write to the other side giving you double the storage. A double-density (DD) disk holds about 180K per side. Unfortunately, only the Atari XF551 disk drive has true DD. Drives from other brands such as the popular Indus GT or Rana could also work with DD. The 1050 drive can read and write 130K per side which means it is in between SD and DD even though it was advertised as DD. This was later called Enhanced Density (ED). The good news is that you can buy DS-DD disks online and format them to SD or DD using any of the drives you want to use. *DOS* 2.5 works with SD, ED, and DD.

Once you have booted DOS, insert the blank disk into the drive and choose the format disk option. This is option 'J' on the *DOS* 2.0 menu that I use with my 810 drive. The formatting doesn't take long. Don't go far.

The **fourth step** is to write DOS to the disk. Once the disk is formatted, you will likely want it to also have your favorite version of

DOS. Most of the DOS versions have an option to write DOS to the disk. In *DOS* 2.0 this is option 'H'.

The **fifth step** is to save a program to the new disk. I went through all these steps recently to make a new disk for the Atari 1020 printer demo. I typed the program in using the *BASIC* cartridge and then saved it to disk using the following BASIC command.

SAVE "D1:PRINTEX1.BAS"

This writes the BASIC program to the disk in drive one. Remember that filenames can't be longer than eight characters. To load the program from disk you can type the following.

LOAD "D1:PRINTEX1.BAS"

Comments. This is a very simple exercise intended for those of you who are doing this for the first time in 30 years or more. I had to refresh my memory the first time back in the saddle. Hopefully writing it down here will make it easier for the returning Atari 8-bit enthusiast. Also, you can always consult one of the many books from the 1980s that have been scanned and provided free online. *Your Atari Computer* (a.k.a the purple book) is a great place to start for a refresher course (see Chapter 3). The text for this book can be found online.

24. Make Floppy Disks Double-Sided (5-10 Minutes)

Prerequisites. For this project, you will need a floppy disk and a notcher. Expect to spend about 5 to 10 minutes notching your disks.

Introduction. When floppy disks first came on the scene, they were single-sided and had a single notch or hole on the right side that you could cover with tape to write-protect the disk. I have included below a scan of a brand-new disk that only has one notch. It didn't take long for someone to discover that you could punch a hole in the other side,  flip the disk over, and write to it. This immediately doubled the capacity of the disk. Of course, the disk makers didn't want us to know this because it reduced sales.

We had a Nibble Notch that was very similar to a hole puncher used to make holes in paper for three-ring notebooks. The Nibble Notch punched rectangular holes and had a guide that helped make sure the hole was punched at the right part of the disk. The Nibble Notch sold for $14.95. There were of course other ways to do this. I provide a few options below. This is still useful today since you can buy new old-stock floppies on eBay.

Instructions. The **first method** is to use a utility knife or other sharp knife to manually cut the notch out of the side of the disk. This works well but has the disadvantage of not looking as nice.

The **second method** is to use a hole punch that you would use to get paper ready for a three-ring binder. These work well, but then you have a disk with one rectangular and one round notch.

The **third method** is to purchase a disk notcher from back in the day. A common brand is Suncom (see below). I have one of these and they work well. They come up on eBay from time to time and usually

sell for about $30-$50. There are several on eBay at the time of writing.

The Nibble Notch is less common and, unfortunately, I lost track of the one I had. I didn't see any of these on eBay when I looked. If you can snag one of these, they are the best way to notch disks because they make a nice clean rectangular cut that looks just like the one from the manufacturer on the right side of the disk.

Comments. Notching disks seems like a trivial thing today. However, disks in the early 1980s were about $1 each which is at least $3 in 2019 dollars. A simple notch would cut the cost of disks in half. This was a big deal and could save a lot of money. Happy notching!

25. Explore Floppy Disk Collections (30-60 Minutes)

Prerequisites. For this project, you will need a collection of floppy disks that you acquired from someone else. Expect to spend at least 30 to 60 minutes exploring the content of disks.

Introduction. One of my favorite things to do with my Atari home computers is explore the contents of my floppy disk collections. I still have my floppies from childhood and have accumulated over 750 floppies from the collections of others (see photo above).

Each of us experienced Atari computers in our own way depending on where we lived, what we had access to, and our financial situation. I love getting large lots of disks because it is a window into history and how that user experienced their Atari 8-bit machine. I have gone through approximately half of my floppy collection. I summarize here some of what I found.

Most of the disks include a variety of pirated games. Many of these come several on a disk and can be selected from a menu upon booting. Pirating was quite common in the early days of home computing, and it wasn't unusual for many people to have a library of pirated games. The people I got my disk lots from had tons of pirated games on disk. Most of the common games are represented in the collection.

The second most prevalent type of disk was from *Antic* magazine that was published from 1982 until 1990. More than 50 of my 750 disks

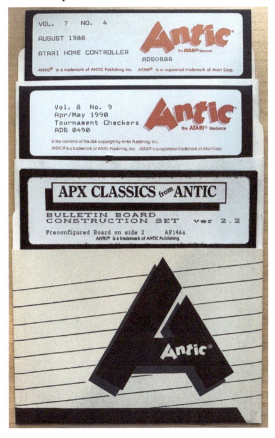

are from *Antic*. I recall getting these in the 1980s and still have many of my original *Antic* disks. They came loaded with the software and games from specific issues of *Antic* and saved you from typing in the programs. *Antic* also acquired some of the Atari Program Exchange (APX) software titles after Atari shut APX down. One of these, the *Bulletin Board Construction Set*, is shown in the photo to the left. Well worth the investment or the effort to pirate them. The ATR files of most of the *Antic* disks can be found online along with much of the software.

There are also quite a few disks with official Atari labels on them. These include Atari formatted disks, master disks (with DOS), *Proofreader Dictionary*, *Translator*, lots of *Bookkeeper* database and data disks, *Home Filing Manager*, and *Atariwriter Plus*. I haven't gone through all of these yet, but it looks like there is quite a bit of content. It should be interesting to see what the previous owners of these disks thought was important enough to database. There are about 20 *Bookkeeper* disks in the collection.

There are also several public domain disks that were distributed by BRE Software out of Fresno, CA. I have disks #19 and #22 (*Print Shop Graphics*), #36 and #38 (*Educational*), #50 (*TextPro*), and #100 and #101 (*Programming*). I don't recall having any of these as a kid, so they are new to me.

I was pleased to find disks for the *Graphical Operating System* (*GOS*) from Total Control Systems. I booted it up successfully and had fun giving it a spin. This was my first time trying this type of OS. The ATR files for these are online if you are interested.

One of the interesting pieces of software I found was the *Bulletin Board Construction Set* (*BBCS*) that was developed by a New Jersey sysop named Scott Brause. I have never run a BBS, but from what I can tell this would have been rewarding.

The Atari demo scene is interesting because the programmers show just what the hardware is capable of. In fact, they have done things with the machines that the Atari engineers and early programmers never dreamed possible. I was pleased to find *The Big Atari 8-Bit Demo* among the many disks. I fired this up and enjoyed trying all the musical and graphical demos. Very impressive stuff! This includes 60K of scrolling text that they claim was a world record for the Atari. The ATR file can be found online.

Finally, I had fun reading some of the word processor files made with *Atariwriter* and other programs. The disks included a Master's thesis and personal letters written to loved ones among other things. I have a screen shot of a portion of one letter below without any direct identifying information.

```
Thanks for the birthday card and
money. I have been saving most of
my money from work and anything
extra is really helpful. I had a
nice birthday. Mom came home and I
had a few friends over.

I've been fairly busy lately. I
have some classes at school this
year that I like already. I'm
exited about graduating this year
and becoming more independent. The
local army recruiter called me on
the 20th (which is the day I cut my
fingers off last year) which was
pretty funny. At least one good
thing came out of that incident
because I won't be drafted. How is
Rover doing? You didn't put her
name or paw print on the card.

FILE:UNCLE                L:21    C:1
PRESS ESC TO RETURN TO MENU
```

Instructions. I recommend seeking out large disk collections locally or on services like eBay (http://ebay.com). They are not cheap on eBay and well worth your time to hunt down locally.

Comments. I have spent numerous hours and days going through this collection of disks. Many will tell you not to waste your time with disks since you can download most of the same software and boot them from an SD drive or SIO2PC. However, I can say that it has been well worth collecting and holding on to these disks. They are very interesting and provide an experience you can't get from an emulator or SD drive. A true window back in time.

I have booted hundreds of disks and estimate that only about 5% or fewer didn't work. That is consistent with my prior experience with floppies and that of others. About 95% of floppies still work today. Another good reason to seek these out!

26. Back Up Floppy Disks to ATR Images (15-30 Minutes)

Prerequisites. For this project, you will need floppy disks, a disk drive, the *Atarimax Prosystem* software, and an SIO2PC. Expect to spend at least 15 to 30 minutes backing up disks.

Introduction. I have at least 750 floppy disks and, amazingly, about 95% of them are still good. However, these don't last forever and can fail if not kept in cool, dry, and dark conditions. It is a good idea to back up to your PC any disks that you don't want to lose. This is very easy to do but does require some special hardware and software. The goal of this task is to backup important floppies to your PC. We will make use of the *Atarimax ProSystem* software for this task (https://www.atarimax.com).

Instructions. The **first step** is to acquire an SIO2PC device to connect your Atari to your PC. This was introduced in Chapter 13. Connect your SIO2PC to your floppy drive and your PC.

The **second step** is to load the floppy you would like to copy into your disk drive. Note that this will not work for copy-protected disks.

The **third step** is to start the *Atarimax ProSystem* software and choose "Create ATR Image from Real Disk" option from the "ATR Functions" menu. This will bring up a new menu titled "Read Disk to ATR Image". First, click on the magnifying glass icon next to the Drive 1 check box to navigate to where you would like to save the ATR image file. Type in the filename you would like to use. Then click the Start button with the green check mark in the lower right of the window. The *ProSystem* will automatically read your disk and copy it to an ATR file in the directory you specified. For my single-density disk this took just less than two minutes to complete.

Comments. This is relatively easy to do and will give you some peace of mind. Be sure and share your ATR files on the Internet Archive (http://archive.org)! Note that you can also use this same software to copy an ATR file from your PC onto a floppy disk, thus reversing the process.

27. Install the *Altirra* Emulator (10-15 Minutes)

Prerequisites. All you need for this project is a PC. Expect to spend about 10 to 15 minutes on the installation and testing.

Introduction. I very much enjoy running software on original Atari home computer hardware. However, it is also nice from time to time to be able to run something on my Windows-based PC. This is especially true for programming where it is much easier and faster to develop and test on a modern PC before deploying to original hardware. The goal of this exercise is to install and try the *Altirra* 8-bit Atari emulator (http://www.virtualdub.org/altirra.html). You might also try *Atari800* (https://atari800.github.io/). I have less experience with this one.

Altirra was programmed by Avery Lee to emulate the Atari 400, 800, XL, and XE computers, as well as the XEGS game system. It was first released in 2009 and has been consistently updated since. Version 3.0 was released in December of 2017. According to the website, "*Altirra* is designed with emulation quality in mind, sometimes over speed and polish. It's designed as a system emulator and debugger instead of a games machine, so there is some setup involved". *Altirra* is licensed under the GNU General Public License (GPL), Version 2.

Instructions. For **step one**, navigate to the *Altirra* website and scroll down to Downloads. You will find there the latest binary and the latest source code. Clicking on the binary link will start the download of a Zip file that contains both 32-bit and 64-bit executables that are compatible with the last several versions of Windows. You can drop the executable right on your desktop and launch it. If you navigate to the System menu and then Profiles you will see a list of 8-bit Atari hardware that you can emulate.

For **step two**, it is time to load a disk image. Atari disk images have the .ATR extension. Many can be found on the Atari Mania website (http://www.atarimania.com/). There is also some Atari 8-bit software on the Internet Archive (http://archive.org). There are others that can be found using Google. Download an ATR file and then boot it from *Altirra* from the File menu and the Boot Image option. This will bring up a dialogue box where you can choose your ATR file. From here you are off and running!

Comments. Altirra has an insane number of options for people who are really in the weeds with the hardware. Fun to play with and explore.

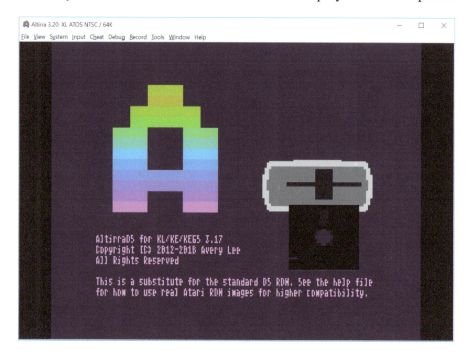

28. Connect an Atari Joystick to Your PC to Use with an Emulator (10-15 Minutes)

Prerequisites. For this project, you will need a USB joystick adapter. Expect to spend about 10 to 15 minutes on the installation.

Introduction. The Atari 400 and 800 were by far the best gaming computers when they hit the market. This was largely due to the awesome ANTIC graphics chip designed by Atari engineers. ANTIC made it possible to put many colors on the screen and enabled Atari's famous player-missile graphics. In addition to the awesome graphics and sound, Atari also had the best joysticks. The Atari joystick (CX40) was so popular that other computer makers such as Commodore included Atari's joystick ports on computers such as the VIC-20. Interestingly, Commodore originally tried to copy the Atari joystick and was taken to court. The details of this can be found on the Wikipedia page for the CX40 joystick (https://en.wikipedia.org/wiki/Atari_CX40_joystick).

I still love Atari joysticks and decided I wanted to be able to connect them to my PC so I could use them to play games on the emulators. Using a keyboard just isn't the same. There are several options available if you poke around online. I went with the 2600-daptor. I have no idea if this is the best one, but it works well for me.

Instructions. Purchase an Atari joystick USB adapter for your PC. I went with the 2600-daptor (http://www.2600-daptor.com) that sells for $25.

Comments. There are several modern Atari-like joysticks with USB cables available online (e.g. Amazon). I am not going to post the links here because the reviews are terrible. I don't have any personal experience with these. I have a box of the original ones and find the adaptor to work well. Enjoy!

29. Save an ATR File from *Altirra* to Your PC (10-15 Minutes)

Prerequisites. All you need for this project is *Altirra*. Expect to spend at least 10 to 15 minutes backing up a few disks.

Introduction. When I first started using the *Altirra* 8-bit emulator, I decided I wanted make ATR floppy disk images that I could then save to my hard disk for later use or to transfer to original hardware using the SIO2PC. For example, I often program in BASIC or assembly language in a text editor or IDE on my PC and then copy and paste the code over to *Altirra* to try using one of the programming languages. Once the code is in *Altirra* and running, I like to save it to an ATR file. I usually copy a blank ATR file with DOS on my PC and have this booted in *Altirra*. The programming language is usually attached as a cartridge. The problem I encountered early on was that I could save to the ATR in *Altirra* but it wasn't saving to the ATR file on my PC and thus was lost when I closed the emulator. I poked around on Atari Age and found a simple solution.

Instructions. According to a helpful post on Atari Age (http://atariage.com), you need to make sure that the ATR file on your PC isn't set to read-only. Some are, depending on the download source. What stumped me was that the file I was working with wasn't set to read-only and still wasn't working. I eventually discovered that the file was blocked by Windows for security reasons. Below the read-only check box in the properties box there was a security message that said "This file came from another computer and might be blocked to help protect this computer". There is a check box next to that message that says Unblock. Clicking that then allowed me to save my work to the ATR file on my PC.

Comments. I hope you find this minor note useful. It is very satisfying to be able to write code on your PC, test it with the emulator, and then immediately boot it up on your Atari to test and run on original hardware. From there you can make a floppy disk, as we discussed in Chapter 23.

30. Edit ATR Images (10-15 Minutes)

Prerequisites. For this project, all you will need is the *Altirra* emulator. Expect to spend at least 10 to 15 minutes editing ATR images.

Introduction. In Chapter 26 I discussed backing up floppy disks to ATR files on a PC using the *Atarimax ProSystem* software. This process can also be reversed allowing you to write ATR files from your PC to a floppy disk. This is all relatively straightforward, but at some point you will want to edit those ATR images on your PC to add new files. Historically, this has been done with the widely-used *makeATR* software. However, there does not seem to be a 64-bit version of this available. Fortunately, ATR images can be edited in *Altirra* using the Disk Explorer option.

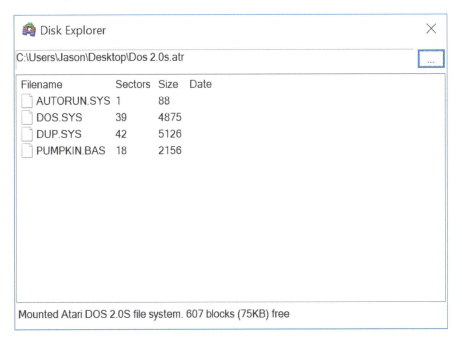

Instructions. For **step one**, download and install the *Altirra* emulator as discussed in Chapter 27.

For **step two**, navigate to the Tools menu and select Disk Explorer. This will bring up a blank window. Click on the dots button under the

X that closes the window. This will bring up a file window where you can select the ATR image you want to edit.

For **step three**, right-clicking on a file in the open ATR image will allow you to rename or delete it. You can also drag and drop files in and out. Any changes are automatically saved to the ATR image file on your computer.

Comments. This is a really easy way to edit ATR files and many of us with PCs use *Altirra* routinely. I confirmed that some BASIC programs that I dropped into the ATR image worked correctly in *Altirra* when run.

There is an Atari Age (http://atariage.com) forum thread from 2012 on this topic.

31. Play *Sea Dragon* (15-30 Minutes)

Prerequisites. For this project, you will need a *Sea Dragon* cassette, disk, or ATR file. Expect to spend at least 15 to 30 minutes having tons of fun.

Introduction. My all-time favorite game on the Atari 8-bit computers was and still is *Sea Dragon*. I still have my original 16K cassette version of this awesome game that I spent many hours loading and playing on my Atari 400 and then 800 computers. *Sea Dragon* was written by Wayne Westmoreland and Terry Gilman for the TRS-80 in 1982. It was ported to the Atari computers by Russ Wetmore who also wrote *Preppie!* for the Atari 8-bits. According to Wikipedia, the game was released into the public domain by Wayne Westmoreland in 1995 and the source code made available by Kevin Savetz on the internet archive in 2015.

I love this game. It is both easy and difficult at the same time. The game play is simple enough. You control a submarine that you can move up and down and forward and backward while the undersea screen scrolls by slowly from right to left. You can fire torpedoes with your fire button, and you have a set amount of oxygen that ticks down requiring you to surface every so often. The goal is to advance to the end while avoiding collisions with the background, objects such as mines and missiles, and lasers from defensive positions. Once you reach the end of the game, you are required to blow up one final objective.

One of the things I really like about this game is the pace. It is a relatively slow-moving game compared to other side-scrollers such as *Defender*. This lets you really focus on strategy and hand-eye coordination. There is just enough randomness to keep you on your toes. It is a pretty easy game to master on the slowest speed. You can crank up the speed for a much faster more arcade-like game play. I am also fond of the graphics. Additionally, they fit the entire game in an amazing 16K so you can play it on your Atari 400!

Instructions. Download the *Sea Dragon* ATR file online and have fun! I have seen the original cassette version with the case on eBay for around $25 to $50.

Interestingly, Atari Age sells a new version of this on cartridge for the Atari 5200. As far as I know, this was never released on cartridge for the 8-bit computers or the 5200 back in the day.

Comments. I played this game more than any other. I recall seeing it advertised in *Compute!* and other magazines and always thinking I was lucky to have an Atari since that version looked the best.

One of my other memories of this game involves my dad, who also loved to play. For some time, the Atari computer was set up in my bedroom, and my dad used to play into the wee hours while I was sleeping for school the next day! I remember waking up in the middle of the night to the infamous beep beep beep of the *Sea Dragon* sonar sounds. I am quite sure the sounds of *Sea Dragon* were burned into my subconscious.

32. Play *Star Raiders* (15-30 Minutes)

Prerequisites. For this project, you will need a *Star Raiders* cartridge, disk, or ROM file. Expect to spend at least 15 to 30 minutes having tons of fun.

Introduction. Star Raiders was released in 1979 along with the Atari 400 and 800 computers. It was a huge success, and the demos in the stores drove numerous 400s and 800s off the shelves. It had very impressive 3D graphics for the time, and people were blown away by the space scenes. It is important to remember that *Star Wars* was in theaters in 1977 and *Star Trek* had been out on TV a decade before. So, everyone was primed for space battle in 3D on the Atari.

The goal of the game is to destroy as many enemy ships as possible. To do this, you navigate a two-dimensional grid where each cell is a sector with enemies in it. Each sector has a base that can be protected by killing the nearby enemies. Navigation has the additional complexity of space objects that must be avoided to prevent damage to your ship. It is a fun game, although it can be tedious at times. There is a good deal of info about the game on Wikipedia. The instructions for the game can be found online.

Instructions. Purchase a *Star Raiders* cartridge or download the ROM file (http://www.atarimania.com) for use with flash cartridge or emulator. The cartridges are quite common and can be found on eBay for about $5 to $10.

Comments. I never had a *Star Raiders* cartridge, for whatever reason, but do remember playing a rented/pirated version of it. If you have never played it, it is worth trying out because of its history and impact on the sales of the Atari 8-bit computers. It is a major part of Atari history!

An interesting bit of trivia is that the Atari 400 was originally planned to be an arcade machine to replace the 2600. As such, the plans did not call for a keyboard. It is my understanding that they added a keyboard specifically so people could play *Star Raiders*.

The source code for *Star Raiders* is available on the Internet Archive (http://archive.org) thanks to Kevin Savetz.

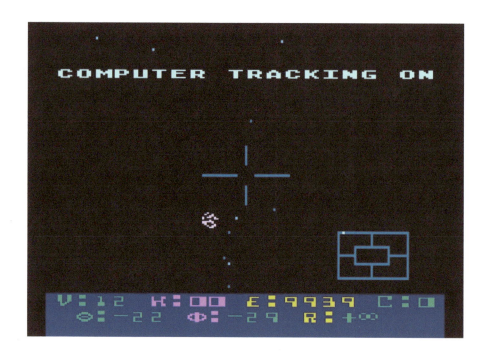

33. Explore Game Easter Eggs (15-60 Minutes)

Prerequisites. For this project, you will need several games including *Dig Dug*, *Super Breakout*, and *Donkey Kong*. Expect to spend at least 15 to 60 minutes playing games.

Introduction. There are several Atari home computer games that have Easter eggs left by programmers. I list here three of these that I personally verified on my own Atari 800 system. The first one, *Dig Dug*, is super easy and quick. The second one, *Super Breakout*, takes just a few seconds. The third one, *Donkey Kong*, took me at least 30 minutes with about 5-6 tries to get it. It requires a relatively complex set of steps compared to *Dig Dug*. The *Donkey Kong* egg was only discovered in 2009 after 26 years and required someone digging through the source code to piece it together.

Instructions. **Dig Dug.** This one is super easy and only takes a few seconds. First, plug your joystick into port #4. Second, press the Option key while holding down the fire button. You will see "The Secret Message" appear on the screen. This one only works with the original release of the *Dig Dug* cartridge. I have two *Dig Dug* cartridges in my collection and fortunately one of them was an original.

Super Breakout. This one is also super easy. Simply press shift-control-I from the main screen to view the egg. You will see "I love Susie and Benjy too" at the bottom of the screen. I have included a screenshot of this from *Altirra* below.

Donkey Kong. The first thing you need to do for the *Donkey Kong* Easter egg is attain a score of 33,XXX and for it to be the high score. Scores of 37,XXX, 73,XXX, and 77,XXX are also supposed to work but I didn't verify these. Don't worry about the hundreds and tens. They can be anything (X). Next, you need to kill off your remaining Marios. The key here is that the last death needs to be due to falling. When the title screen comes back, press the option key three times to set it to difficulty four. Wait for the cut scene with *Donkey Kong* jumping on the beams. When this is over, the title screen will reappear with the initials LMD at the bottom. These are the initials for the programmer Landon M. Dyer. This is the egg! I will list a tip in the comments below for accomplishing this. If you want to figure out how to do this yourself then skip that section.

Comments. What I learned is that you need to sandbag your score on *Donkey Kong* in the first several levels. In other words, let the time run down on a few of them and maybe avoid some of the prizes. If you don't do this you will likely end up with 33,XXX points on the pie factory level and this one is difficult to finish on. By sandbagging your score you can get by this one and hit 33,XXX on the elevator level, which is next. This is the ideal one to end on because it is easy to kill Mario off by falling.

34. Read the Book *Atari BASIC* (1-2 Hours)

Prerequisites. For this project, you will need a copy or PDF of the book *Atari BASIC,* by Albrecht et al. (1979). Expect to spend at least one to two hours if you are learning *Atari BASIC* for the first time.

Introduction. My first two books were *Your Atari Computer* and *Atari BASIC.* They are still a great way to get familiar with the Atari 400 and 800 if you are just getting started or need a refresher. I worked my way through much of the *Atari BASIC* book when I was teaching myself BASIC back in the early 1980s. It is a very gentle introduction that was perfect for me as a kid.

The first several chapters help get you oriented to using the Atari. Chapter 3 then introduces variables and branching. Chapter 4 goes over IF-THEN statements, while Chapter 5 covers DATA and READ statements. The book goes on to cover FOR-NEXT loops, indexing variables, strings, and finally graphics and sound. You won't be programming games with player-missile graphics after reading this, but you will learn the fundamentals of *Atari BASIC* that are needed to get into the more advanced topics that are covered in the next few chapters.

One of the nice things about this book is that it provides a self-test at the end of each chapter where you can evaluate your knowledge. For example, at the end of the chapter on FOR-NEXT loops you are asked to show what will be printed if you run the following program:

```
10 P=1:FOR K=1 TO 4:P=P*K:NEXT K:PRINT P
```

The answer to this one is of course 24.

Instructions. Purchase a copy of *Atari BASIC* from eBay or another online seller. It is widely available and at the time of this post sells for around $10 to $20 used. It is also available online from Atari Archives and the Internet Archive. There is also an updated version for the XL series of computers.

Comments. This book was very popular and sold many copies. I was able to find some information about the authors online. For example, Bob Albrecht has a Wikipedia entry. Leroy Finkel and Jerald Brown authored several books, including one for the TRS-80.

35. Read the Book *De Re Atari* (1-2 Hours)

Prerequisites. For this project, you will need a copy or PDF of the book *De Re Atari* by Crawford et al. (1982). Expect to spend at least one to two hours or more with this book.

Introduction. When the Atari 400 and 800 computers were released in 1979, they were a closed system. That is, only Atari personnel knew the details of the hardware that were necessary for the development of software. This gave Atari a monopoly on the system

thus eliminating third-party software. This was one in a long series of errors that Atari made in their business plan. A few years later, they realized their mistake and set about to correct it. One of the first things they did was write a series of articles detailing the key aspects of Atari hardware that were needed by programmers. This was published in book form as *De Re Atari* in 1982. Some of the articles appeared in magazines such as *Compute!* and *BYTE* prior to 1982. There was one on player-missile graphics by Chris Crawford

that was published in *Compute!* in 1981 (Issue 8, page 66). Interestingly, *De Re Atari* was sold through the Atari Program Exchange (APE) as an unbound set of pages with holes to put them in a three-ring binder.

De Re Atari covers a lot of key topics for Atari programming in BASIC and assembly language, including details of the ANTIC chip that are needed for display lists and display list interrupts, for example. This is a must-read for anyone serious about learning to program on the Atari 8-bit computers. Consider it an essential reference for the next few chapters.

Instructions. You can purchase new old stock of *De Re Atari* in print from Best Electronics (http://www.best-electronics-ca.com) for $29.95. Search for it on their page. This is what I did. I have mine in an original three-ring binder from Atari. I also have my original copy in a binder from my childhood. It is also freely available in web form from Atari Archives (http:// atariarchives.org) and as a PDF from the Internet Archive (archive.org).

Comments. The book had a huge impact on Atari programming back in the early 1980s. In fact, you can see authors of other books and magazines closely paraphrasing what was said in *De Re Atari* indicating what an important reference it was. I can always tell when an author is doing this.

One can only wonder how making the Atari 8-bits open from the beginning would have boosted their competitive edge. Having tons of third-party software and games would have helped establish their computer line as the one to own. It certainly would have helped their battle with Commodore. Those few lost early years from 1979 to 1981 were crucial.

There is a Wikipedia page for *De Re Atari* for readers wanting more details about this book, how and why it was written, and some of its content (https://en.wikipedia.org/wiki/De_Re_Atari).

As Atari guru Bill Wilkinson said, "I must heartily recommend that every serious Atari programmer trade in his or her left thumb, if necessary, for a copy of this book".

36. Try GTIA Graphics Modes in BASIC (30-60 Minutes)

Prerequisites. For this project, you will need BASIC. Expect to spend at least 30 to 60 minutes typing in and running programs.

Introduction. When the Atari 400 and 800 first shipped, they included the Color Television Interface Adaptor or CTIA chip that creates the signal that goes to the television for display. The CTIA is controlled by the ANTIC microprocessor that includes an instruction set and a program called the "display list" that dictates what graphics modes will be used for each line on the screen. The display list, and the information that will be drawn on the screen, are written to memory and then the ANTIC sends that to the CTIA for display. This is all described on page 1-1 of the wonderful book *De Re Atari* (Chapter 35).

A second chip called the Graphic Television Interface Adaptor or GTIA had the same functionality of the CTIA, but with several additional graphics modes. It wasn't quite ready for the initial shipments of Atari 400 and 800 computers but was introduced in the early 1980s such that nearly all the 8-bit computers you come across today have the more advanced GTIA chip. I recall reading about the GTIA in one of the computer magazines back in the day and wondering whether my Atari had the newer chip. I tested this by typing in some BASIC programs that called on the GTIA's extra graphics modes. Indeed, my Atari had the GTIA and I was impressed with the additional capabilities. The goal of this project is to try some BASIC programs that use the extra GTIA modes.

Instructions. The book *The Creative Atari,* by Small et al. (1983) has a chapter on GTIA graphics with 11 BASIC programs you can type in and run. Each one is between about 10 and 50 lines of code and can be typed in quickly or cut and paste directly from the online source into an emulator. I outline one of these that you can download and try.

Step one. Open the *Altirra* emulator and load any version of BASIC.

Step two. Open GTIA-demo.txt from your text editor and copy the text to your clipboard. You can find this file on the Atari Projects website (atariprojects.org) or by a Google search on the filename.

Step three. Click on the View tab of *Altirra* and choose the Paste Text option from the bottom of the list. *Altirra* will slowly paste the text into the BASIC command line. It is important to keep focus on the *Altirra* window, or the paste will stop and it will lose some characters.

Step four. Once finished with the paste, you can LIST to see the program and then RUN to see the result. See the screenshot below for what this program draws.

Comments. The GTIA effects are impressive because they have mode shades of one color allowing for more effective 3-D effects like the Brass demo (see screenshot below). These extra graphics modes are fun to play with and were used in some games. I still recall the first time I gave some of these a try in the early 1980s. I was very impressed. There is an article in *Compute!* from 1982 about the new GTIA chips (Issue 26, Page 124). There is also a GTIA article from 1983 in *Antic* magazine (Volume 2, Number 1). This last article includes a nice demo you can try.

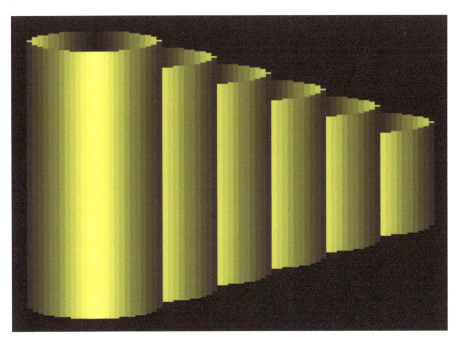

37. Make a Playfield in BASIC Using Redefined Character Sets (30-60 Minutes)

Prerequisites. For this project, you will need the BASIC programming language. Expect to spend at least 30 to 60 minutes trying and understanding the program provided. You will need additional time to try your own redefined character set.

Introduction. I programmed a game called *Gene Medic* (http://genemedic.org) in assembly language for the Atari 2600 in 2017 and am interested in porting it to the Atari 800 (see screenshot below). I am starting this process using BASIC and may also do an assembly language version once I have that working. I have had a good time diving back into BASIC and learning graphics tricks and techniques that I didn't learn, or didn't learn well, back in the day. BASIC on the Atari 8-bit computer is so much easier than programming in assembly for the 2600.

I am starting with a simple playfield drawn entirely in graphics mode 0 (ANTIC mode 2) with characters. Graphics mode 0 is one of the three text modes. This one allows 40 8x8 pixel characters to be drawn across the screen with 24 total lines. This is the same graphics mode that the *Atari BASIC* cartridge and the *Memo Pad* use. My first

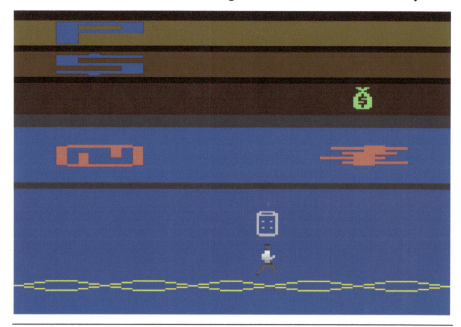

thought was that I could draw the entire playfield for *Gene Medic* in this text mode and use the character set provided for the shapes needed. There are two problems with this. First, I discovered that the shapes provided in the character set couldn't be used to draw some of the shapes I needed. Second, graphics 0 is limited to one color for the background and the same color for the characters with a different luminance (brightness) that gives it contrast. The first problem is easily overcome by redefining the character set to include the shapes I need. More about this below. The second issue cannot be overcome here and will be addressed in a later chapter (39) on mixing graphics modes with display lists. For now, I will just go with the color limitations to illustrate a playfield drawn only with character sets. The playfield I will ultimately use for my game will be more sophisticated.

I have read several sources on character sets. My favorite is "The Beginner's Guide to Character Sets" on page 46 of the book *The Creative Atari,* by Small et al. (1983). I modified their program #28 for the demo. The Atari ASCII character set (i.e. ATASCII) consists of 128 characters, shapes, and symbols that can be placed anywhere on the 40x24 graphics 0 text screen using the POSITION X,Y command followed by a PRINT "A" or PRINT CHR$(65) command in BASIC. Note that the next 128 characters in the set are each coded by eight bytes. Thus, the complete character set occupies 8*128=1024 bytes of memory, or one complete page. Websites with the characters listed alongside their ATASCII number and internal reference number can be found online on web pages such as Atari Archives (e.g. https://www.atariarchives.org/mapping/appendix10.php). The internal reference number is important for pointing to characters in memory and is what I use in my code below. Note that the first 20 or so ATASCII characters are shapes that can be directly used to draw a simple playfield. As I mentioned above, these shapes did not have enough variety for my playfield. This means that I needed to define some new characters for my screen. The ability to define new characters was a clear advantage of the Atari over other similar computers from the late 1970s and early 1980s.

I found redefining a character set to be fun. The first thing you need to know is that the character set is located in the ROM where it can't be modified. You must first copy the character set to RAM where it can then be changed. Once changed, you can tell the Atari to use this as the source of characters, thus bypassing the fixed set in ROM. This

---

is all pretty straightforward and explained clearly in *The Creative Atari* chapter I mentioned above. I decided to modify 10 letters, A through J, to make the shapes I needed. The A character has internal reference number 33 with B as 34, C as 35, etc. Each character is defined by an 8x8 bitmap that is read line by line from the top down. For a _ character I used DATA 0,0,0,0,0,0,0,255 where the first seven 0s indicate blank lines for the top seven rows of the 8x8 matrix and the 255 is the decimal value of the binary number 11111111 for the bottom row making the _ character. These data statements are read using the READ statement and then poked into eight consecutive memory locations corresponding to the character being modified. In my new character set I changed "I" to "_". So now when I use PRINT "I" a "_" will appear on the screen.

An important issue to consider is that loading the character set from ROM to RAM is slow in BASIC and there is a noticeable pause of about 5-10 seconds until it completes. I have included a machine language routine from page 59 of the book *Atari Graphics and Arcade Game Design,* by Stanton and Pinal (1984) that is much faster. I present first the code written entirely in BASIC below followed by the code with the machine language routine for comparison. I will also provide fully commented code in the comments section.

Instructions. The following instructions are for running the character set playfield code in the *Altirra* emulator. You can of course type the code in by hand and run it on original hardware with BASIC.

Step one. Open the *Altirra* emulator and load BASIC. I used *Turbo BASIC XL.* You can also load the built-in BASIC from *Altirra* from the File->Attach Special Cartridge menu.

Step two. Open char-set-redefine.txt from your text editor and copy the text to your clipboard. You can find this file on the Atari Projects website (atariprojects.org) or by a Google search on the filename.

Step three. Click on the View tab of *Altirra* and choose the Paste Text option from the bottom of the list. *Altirra* will slowly paste the text into the BASIC command line. It is important to keep focus on the *Altirra* window, or the paste will stop and it will lose some characters.

Step four. Once finished with the paste, you can LIST to see the program and then RUN to see the result. Note that there is a 5-10 second pause after you RUN while the character set is loaded from ROM to RAM.

Step five. Repeat with char-set-redefine-ml.txt that includes the machine language code. Compare the speed. You should choose Cold Boot from the System menu to reboot the Atari before loading the new code. A Warm Boot will reset BASIC without purging the code from memory. You can also find this file on the Atari Projects website or by a Google search on the filename.

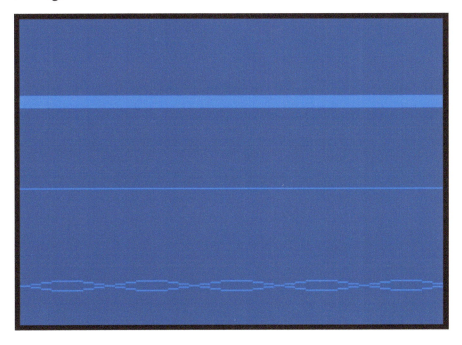

Comments. I would encourage you to play with the code to develop your own character set. My simple playfield shown just above is a first attempt to approximate the one I did on the Atari 2600 (see figure further up). In *Gene Medic*, the playfield is a cell with the thick horizontal line representing the cell membrane. The thin line represents the nuclear membrane. At the bottom is a double-stranded DNA molecule in the nucleus of the cell. Note that the background is dark blue (SETCOLOR 2,9,2) while the characters are all light blue (SETCOLOR 1,9,9).

I have also prepared a heavily commented version of the BASIC code with the machine language routine to make it easier for you to learn how this works so you can make your own playfield. The code for this is in the file char-set-redefine-ml-comments.txt that you can find on Atari Projects website or by Google search. I will discuss display lists in a later chapter (39) to extend this work and give it more functionality by mixing graphics modes. Modifying display lists is an important and useful skill for making Atari 8-bit computer games. The next chapter includes an example applied to making some Halloween pumpkins.

38. Draw Halloween Pumpkins in BASIC Using Redefined Character Sets (10-15 Minutes)

Prerequisites. For this project, you will need the BASIC programming language. Expect to spend at least 10 to 15 minutes trying the program provided. You will need additional time to try your own redefined character set.

Introduction. When Halloween was approaching, I went on to the web to see if there were some fun BASIC programs designed specifically for the haunted day. Unfortunately, I didn't find any. There are a few graphics demos of scary images, but I couldn't find any source code. So, I decided to design a pumpkin and implement it in BASIC using the redefined character set method introduced in the previous chapter.

The first thing I needed to do was design the pumpkin pixel-by-pixel. I did this by mapping out a series of 8x8 grids in *Powerpoint* that

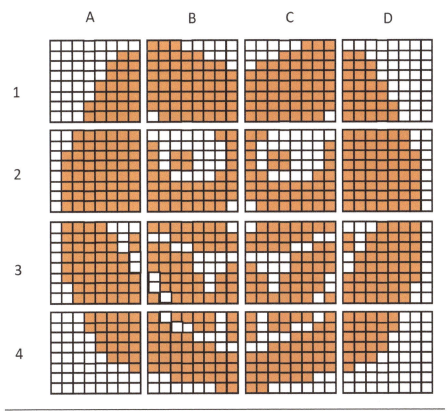

each represents a letter or character that would get replaced by the new design.

This is tedious but is exactly how it was done back in the day. Of course, back then we used graph paper. To draw my pumpkin, we need to redefine 16 characters. I redefined characters A through P. I did this column by column. For example, grid A-1 represents the letter A while A-2 represents B, etc.

The next step is to convert each 8x8 grid to a vector of eight decimal values that are calculated from the binary representation of each row. Here, you start with the leftmost pixel as 128, the next one as 64, etc. with the rightmost pixel of each row as a 1. In other words, think of each row as a binary array with 1s where the pixels are lit up and 0s where they are blank. You then convert this binary number to a decimal number. The value for first row in A-1 is a decimal 0 while the second row is a 3. The next one is a 7. So, the decimal vector representing A-1 is 0, 3, 7, 7, 15, 15, 31, 31. The decimal vector for A-2 is 63, 63, 127, 127, 127, 127, 127, 127. These are presented in the code as DATA statements and read into the memory locations where the bitmaps for letters A through P are stored (we move all the characters from ROM to RAM for editing).

I used Graphics 2+16 here for the big block letters. Note a key difference from the character set code I presented in the previous chapter is that we use PRINT #6 statements here instead of just PRINT

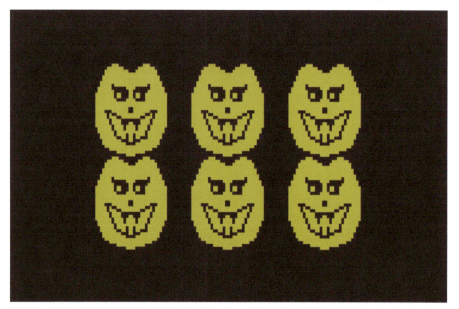

to print the characters on the screen. PRINT is only for Graphics 0. I repeated the pumpkins six times across the screen just for fun.

Instructions. **Step one.** Open the *Altirra* emulator and load BASIC. I used *Turbo BASIC XL*. You can also load the built-in BASIC from *Altirra* from the File->Attach Special Cartridge menu.

Step two. Open char-set-pumpkin.txt from your text editor and copy the text to your clipboard. You can find this file on the Atari Projects website (atariprojects.org) or by a Google search on the filename.

Step three. Click on the View tab of *Altirra* and choose the Paste Text option from the bottom of the list. *Altirra* will slowly paste the text into the BASIC command line. It is important to keep focus on the *Altirra* window, or the paste will stop and it will lose some characters.

Step four. Once finished with the paste, you can LIST to see the program and then RUN to see the result.

Comments. I hope you find this additional example of using redefined character sets useful. Happy Halloween!

39. Learn About Display List Interrupts in BASIC (1-2 Hours)

Prerequisites. For this project, you will need the BASIC programming language. Expect to spend at least one to two hours trying and understanding the program provided. You will need additional time to try your own display list interrupts.

Introduction. Atari was far ahead of its competitors when it was released with superior graphics. This was largely due to the ANTIC chip that served as a graphics processor with its own instruction set and program for drawing the screen (i.e. the display list). The display list makes it possible to mix graphics modes giving the programmer great flexibility for drawing screens with both text and graphics. Unfortunately, each graphics mode was limited to a small number of colors, despite the Atari having 256 total colors to choose from with the GTIA chip. For example, graphics 0 is a text mode that can display 40 columns by 24 rows of characters with only two colors for the background and the text. Graphics 0 is even more limited because the color of the text is dependent on the background color and thus cannot be set independently. Fortunately, the Atari engineers built in a remedy for these restrictions. The display list interrupt (DLI) makes it possible to control the background color of every line drawn on the screen. This is generally called a raster interrupt or horizontal blank interrupt. The Atari 8-bit home computers were the first to do this.

Learning about DLIs is difficult for several reasons. First, it is used in conjunction with other features of the Atari, including display lists and player-missile graphics that each take time to learn and understand. Second, there are several details that must be taken care of in the right order to implement a DLI. Third, the code that runs during the interrupt to set the parameters of the next scan line to be drawn must be written in assembly language since it is run during the horizontal blank which has precious few CPU cycles and thus must be executed quickly. Finally, there is no one authoritative source on DLIs. Each source I have read explains it differently and leaves out key details that must be collated to have a complete understanding of the process. It took me a few weeks to gain a basic understanding of DLIs, and I will try to convey what I have learned here. Please know that I don't yet consider myself an expert, but I think I have learned enough to help others get started more efficiently. Unfortunately, this is one of those more complex topics that requires a bit of work and frustration to become an expert. There is no easy way to learn DLIs.

The first thing you need to know is that the ANTIC chip is busy working with the GTIA to draw the screen while the CPU is busy with the computations required by the software. This was a huge advance over the Atari 2600 that lacked a graphics chip, resulting in a CPU that was burdened with drawing the screen one scan line at a time. The only time the 2600 CPU had to do in-game computations was during the horizontal blank (a brief pause) at the end of each scan line and the vertical blank (a longer pause) when the last of the 192 scan lines comprising the screen was completed. With the 8-bit computers, the ANTIC gets its marching orders from its display list that is created automatically when a graphics mode is specified in BASIC or a custom display list with multiple graphics modes is created. With the display list in hand, ANTIC goes about its business drawing the screen within the limitations of each graphics mode it is asked to draw. The DLI essentially tells the ANTIC to signal to the CPU that there is a nonmaskable interrupt (NMI). This happens when ANTIC gets to the end of the current scan line. The CPU stops what it is doing and then runs or services an assembly language routine you provide at a specified memory address. This bit of code changes the graphics registers controlling the display. Once the code is executed, the CPU goes back to what it was doing. The ANTIC then uses the new graphics settings on the next scan lines until another DLI is called. Calling a DLI every mode line means that you can give each line a different color. This makes it possible to have 24 different colors for each of the 24 different graphics 0 mode lines (eight scan lines per mode line) that make up the 192 scan lines of the screen. Fun!

I am not going to repeat all the details from the various sources here. Instead I will make some reading recommendations and then provide below instructions for running an example program I cobbled together to illustrate the DLI. I tried to make the program as simple as possible, but that was hard to do as I will explain below in the comments. The first source I recommend reading is from a series of Atari Tutorials that appeared in *BYTE* magazine. These tutorials were based on the chapters of *De Re Atari*. I read somewhere that this was an attempt by Atari to introduce its machines and their programming advantages to a wider audience. Seems like a good move. Tutorial part

4 in the December 1981 issue of *BYTE* covers DLIs. There are several other sources of information about DLIs. I recommend the *De Re Atari* chapter.

Instructions. The following instructions are for running the example DLI code in *Altirra*. You can of course type the code in by hand or save it to a floppy and run it on original hardware with BASIC.

Step one. Open *Altirra* and load BASIC. I used *Turbo BASIC XL*. You can also load the built-in BASIC from *Altirra* from the File->Attach Special Cartridge menu.

Step two. Open the file DLI-example.txt in your text editor or web browser and copy the text to your clipboard. You can find this file on the Atari Projects website (atariprojects.org) or by a Google search on the filename.

Step three. Click on the View tab of *Altirra* and choose the Paste Text option from the bottom of the list. *Altirra* will slowly paste the text into the BASIC command line. It is important to keep focus on the *Altirra* window, or the paste will stop and it will lose some characters.

Step four. Once finished with the paste, you can LIST to see the program and then RUN to see the result.

Below is a screen shot from *Altirra* showing two alternating colors in graphics 0. Normally you get only one. You can change the color

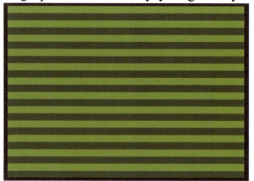

codes in lines 230 and 240 for whatever color you want.

Comments. Even though I read all the sources carefully and pieced together what I thought would be a working DLI example I had problems getting it to work correctly. I tried lots of different variations with no luck and eventually phoned a friend and posted for help on the Atari Age 8-bit programming forum. You can see my Atari Age forum post and the several responses here (https://atariage.com/forums/topic/285311-dli-help-thanks/). As you can see, I missed some key details in my readings. A bit complicated as I mentioned earlier in the post. A version of the code with comments can be found online under the filename DLI-example-comments.txt.

40. Learn About Player-Missile Graphics in BASIC (30-60 Minutes)

Prerequisites. For this project, you will need the BASIC programming language. Expect to spend at least 30 to 60 minutes trying and understanding the program provided. You will need additional time to try your own player-missile graphics.

Introduction. Player-missile (PM) graphics helped make the Atari the premier arcade and graphics machine in its day. A key feature of PM graphics is the ability to draw players and missiles on the screen that are independent of the background or playfield graphics. This is a very powerful feature but can also be difficult to understand and program. Think of PM graphics as a second Atari graphics system that lives on top of the standard one used to draw objects and characters on the screen. There are a few different books and magazines from the 1980s that explain PM graphics to varying degrees of success. I have read a number of these, and each is a little different. I present here one approach that makes sense to me. I encourage you to read several different sources and descriptions and find one that resonates.

One of the challenges is that the Atari is set up to move players horizontally with ease by writing the X position to a horizontal position register that is checked by the CTIA/GTIA. This is done with free cycles that are left over after it has kept track of the horizontal position of the scan line being drawn. However, positioning players vertically on the Y axis is slow in BASIC because the memory mapping of the player is upside down, requiring PEEKs and POKEs to move the image in the right direction. I have tried this myself and it is indeed very slow. There are two general options. The first is to write your code in fast assembly language. The second is to call from BASIC a routine for player movement written in assembly language. The assembly code is provided in DATA statements and written to memory where it is then called and executed when needed. A variation on this approach is to store it in strings which are fast to manipulate. I personally am less fond of the string approach, but I think that is because I am more familiar with executing assembly code from memory.

The player movement routine that I like is provided on page 164 of *Compute's First Book of Atari Graphics* (1982). This nice method takes advantage of the vertical blank interrupt (VBLANK) after the drawing of the screen has been completed. The Atari naturally pauses to do some housekeeping before the screen starts drawing again. Atari built-in the capability to run some assembly code during this VBLANK. So, we can load up our player position code into memory and then tell the Atari to look for it and execute it during the VBLANK. The nice thing about this approach is that we only need to do this once as an initialization step in the program. The Atari takes care of the rest and executes the position changes 60 time per second every time the screen is drawn. This makes this positioning code very fast and efficient.

I have taken the program provided on page 170-171 of *Compute's First Book of Atari Graphics* and modified it to my own understanding. Below is the basic flow of the program. I refer the reader to the book text for a more detailed description. The instructions below outline how to obtain and run the code in the file PM-demo-VBlank.txt that can be found online.

Lines 100-130. We first set aside 16 pages of memory for the PM graphics (lower 8 pages - 8 pages * 256 bytes per page = 2048 bytes for single-line resolution) and the display list and screen display (higher 8 pages - handles up to GRAPHICS 5) just below the top of available RAM (i.e. RAMTOP). We then calculate the memory address where the PM graphics will go (pages * 256 bytes per page). There are 160 pages on an Atari 800 with 48K of RAM. We subtracted 16 pages here to leave 144. So, our PMBASE memory start address is 144 * 256 or 36,864. There is a table in Chapter 3 of *Atari Assembly Language Guide* that lists the memory needed for each graphics model. You will need to set aside more than 8 pages of memory for GRAPHICS modes 6-8.

Lines 200-240. The next step is to initialize the graphics. This is important because the GRAPHICS statement must come right after the top of RAM reset. This is because the display memory is set to a point just below the top of memory. Note that, as stated in the book chapter, you must reserve more than 16 pages of RAM if GRAPHICS 6-8 are to be used. We then set the background color to black, turn off the cursor, and set the player color to green.

Lines 300-320. This bit of code sets the memory addresses of the player X and Y coordinates and the initial position.

Lines 400-470. This is the code that reads in the assembly code in the DATA statements to page 6 of memory (1536 = 6 * 256). Some memory is then cleared out with 0s followed by the code that reads the player graphics in (line 440). The next lines set up the PM graphics. Line 470 calls some assembly code that tells the OS to include our movement routine as part of the VBLANK.

Lines 500-520. This code prints a title on the screen.

Lines 600-660. This code is the main loop of the program that moves the player. Here, we POKE the player X and Y coordinates into a memory address that is used by our VBLANK movement routine. The player movement subroutine that reads the joystick is called.

Lines 700-810. This code reads the joystick and increments or decrements the player X and Y coordinates. It also checks the position to wrap the player around the edges of the screen.

Lines 1000-1100. These DATA statements contain the code for the assembly language routines that move the player during the VBLANK.

Lines 2000-2010. This DATA statement contains the line by line shape code for the player. A Star Wars-like tie fighter is drawn.

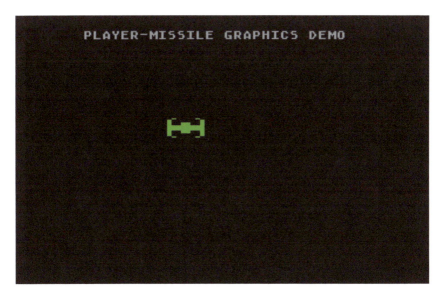

As I said, there are several references for PM graphics that you might consult as you learn. You should start with *De Re Atari* (see Chapter 4). There is a BASIC program there you can type in and run to see how slow PM graphics are without assembly language movement routines. I then recommend Chapter 5 of *Compute's First Book of Atari Graphics*. *The Creative Atari* has some nice details you might not find elsewhere (see page 39). I found Chapter 5 of *Atari Graphics and Arcade Design* to be a good reference. The *Atari Assembly Language Guide* has some good info in Chapter 3, including a table with the number of bytes taken up by each graphics mode. *The Computer Animation Primer* has a nice chapter on page 239. There is a book called *Player-Missile Graphics in BASIC,* although I didn't find it as helpful. There are also a few magazine articles you can find using Google.

Instructions. The following instructions are for running the example PM code in the *Altirra* emulator. You can of course type the code in by hand and run it on original hardware with BASIC or boot the ATR file and load the BASIC file using SIO2PC.

Step one. Open *Altirra* and load BASIC. I used *Turbo BASIC XL*. You can also load the built-in BASIC from *Altirra* from the File-> Attach Special Cartridge menu.

Step two. Open the file PM-demo-VBlank.txt in your text editor or web browser and copy the text to your clipboard. You can find this file on the Atari Projects website (atariprojects.org) or by a Google search on the filename.

Step three. Click on the View tab of *Altirra* and choose the Paste Text option from the bottom of the list. *Altirra* will slowly paste the text into the BASIC command line. It is important to keep focus on the *Altirra* window, or the paste will stop and it will lose some characters.

Step four. Once finished with the paste, you can LIST to see the program and then RUN to see the result. Above is a screen shot from *Altirra*.

Comments. Use the demo and try different settings to learn how this works. One of the things I noticed is that the demo ran much more slowly on *Atari BASIC*. The speed was much better on *BASIC XL*, *Turbo BASIC XL*, and on *Altirra BASIC*. Big difference!

41. Read the Book *Breakout: How Atari 8-Bit Computers Defined a Generation* (3-6 Hours)

Prerequisites. For this project, you will need the book *Breakout* by Jamie Lendino. Expect to spend at least three to six hours to read the entire book.

Introduction. Learning about Atari history and trivia on the web can be difficult since the information is fragmented across multiple different web pages and sources. Fortunately, there are authors who are willing to take the time to collate much of this information into very useful books. *Breakout* is a marvelous book that summarizes the history of Atari 8-bit home computers with coverage of hardware and software including a number of games. There is some good commentary about some of the mistakes Atari made and how, had things gone differently, they could have dominated the home computer market in the early 1980s. The book also covers topics such as emulation and collecting. I highly recommend it. It is an easy and fun read and will leave you with a great foundation for enjoying your Atari 8-bit hobby.

Instructions. Breakout: How Atari 8-Bit Computers Defined a Generation by Jamie Lendino is available in paperback from Amazon for $17.99. It is also available on Kindle for $9.99.

Comments. A must-have for any Atari 8-bit enthusiast. Note that about half the book summarizes some of the popular games for the 8-bit series. You can get through the other half the book in about three hours or so.

42. Read the Book *Atari Inc.: Business is Fun* (10-15 Hours)

Prerequisites. For this project, you will need the book *Atari Inc.*, by Marty Goldberg and Curt Vendel. This book is over 800 pages and will take at least 10-15 hours to get through if you read the whole thing. There are a lot of photos so the actual number of pages that need to be read is probably less than 500.

Introduction. This book is a tour de force in Atari stories and history and is a must-have for any Atari enthusiast's bookshelf. As Curt Vendel states in the Foreword, the stories behind Atari are as important as the products themselves. Atari is an amazing journey from start to finish. The people that created and drove Atari to the most important video game company of its time all have wonderful memories to share.

This book covers the early history of Atari up through the mid-1980s. This was the time period when the Atari 2600 console and the Atari 8-bit computers were released. The book was purposefully written in a very informal style that makes it easy and fun to read. In addition to the great historical accounts and stories, there are lots of photos and scans of rare documents you will not find on the web. These are tons of fun to look at.

Instructions. Atari Inc.: Business is Fun by Marty Goldberg and Curt Vendel is available in paperback from Amazon for $29.99. It is also available on Kindle for $11.99.

Comments. Note that much of the book focuses on the early days of Atari. There is a bit less on the home consoles and computers. Thanks to Goldberg and Vendel for all their hard work to assemble and synthesize all this information. It is very much appreciated!

43. Read the Book *Terrible Nerd* (3-6 Hours)

Prerequisites. All you need for this project is the book *Terrible Nerd*, by Kevin Savetz. Expect to spend at least three to six hours reading the book.

Introduction. Many of us grew up with Atari home computers in the 1980s. I certainly did with my Atari 400 and then 800. Those were great times and many of us were inspired in our careers by our experience growing up at a time when home computing was new and unfolding before our eyes. I am sure many of us could write interesting books about that time and how it impacted our current selves. As such, I was very excited to purchase and read Kevin Savetz's book about his experience growing up with Atari and Apple computers. He talks about playing video games, learning to code, and the craft of pirating software, which was quite common back in those days. This book was so much fun to read and parts paralleled my own life. I highly recommend it. It is an easy and fun read and will stimulate many of your own memories with vintage computers.

Instructions. Terrible Nerd by Kevin Savetz is available in paperback from Amazon for $14.99. It is also available for free on Kindle.

Comments. Kevin Savetz is well-known in the Atari 8-bit computer community as one of the three hosts of the *ANTIC* podcast (see Chapter 45). He is very active in the retro-computing scene and has made significant contributions of scanned material to the Internet Archive. Here is his website if you would like more information: https://www.savetz.com.

44. Listen to the *Floppy Days* Podcast (1-4 Hours)

Prerequisites. All you need for this project is a web browser or podcast app. Expect to spend at least one to four hours per episode or collection of episodes on a specific topic.

Introduction. The *Floppy Days* podcast was founded by Randall Kindig in 2013 and has been going strong every year for the last six years. Randy's goal is to cover as many vintage computers as possible and, so far, he has been extremely successful. His podcasts have covered all the common classics, including the Apple, Atari,  Commodore, Sinclair, Texas Instruments, and TRS-80 models. He has also covered some of the very early computers, such as the Altair 8800 and some of the more obscure computers, like the HP-85. His coverage usually starts out with an overview of the technical specifications, followed by a review of the peripherals and available sources of information. This is an amazingly valuable resource. He also does some interviews with experts and covers events such as the Vintage Computer Festivals that are held each year around the USA and Europe (see Chapter 50).

Randy, an Atari enthusiast and expert, did a great job covering the 400 and 800 computers in three episodes. I have listed these below for your listening pleasure. It is a great introduction for those just getting into the hobby or if you are an expert in need of a refresher.

Instructions. All of the *Floppy Days* podcast episodes are available online (http://floppydays.libsyn.com/). There are three episodes that cover the details of the Atari 8-bit computers.

The **first episode** covers the technical details of the Atari 400 and 800. This is episode 33, published in May of 2015.

The **second episode** covers websites, books, magazines, and other resources. This is episode 36, published in April of 2015.

The **third episode** covers modern upgrades and connectivity to modern computers. This is episode 40, published in May of 2015.

Comments. This is one of my favorite podcasts. Randy has a nice easy-going podcasting style that I really like. I have enjoyed listening to all the episodes including those about non-Atari computers. I have learned a lot from Randy's excellent, detail-oriented coverage. His theme song is cool too. Be sure and check it out!

45. Listen to the *ANTIC Atari 8-Bit Podcast* (1-2 Hours)

Prerequisites. All you need for this project is a web browser or podcast app. Expect to spend at least one to two hours per episode.

Introduction. There is so much to learn about Atari home computers. This is a lifetime hobby that never grows old. There is endless material in retro magazines, books, archives, and web pages to read and digest. However, there is nothing like listening to experts discuss and debate the finer points of Atari history, hardware, and software. Fortunately, there are a number of retro-computing podcasts that satisfy this curiosity. Some, like the *Retro Computing Roundtable* (RCR), cover all old computers, including Atari. I really like this one. Another is *Retrobits* that, while no longer active, has great material from across the computing spectrum. I also really like *Floppy Days* which is a generalist retro-computing podcast with some good Atari content (see Chapter 44). However, for the Atari lover, nothing beats the *ANTIC Atari 8-Bit Podcast* that is 100% dedicated to Atari 8-bit home computers.

ANTIC was founded in 2013 and is hosted by Brad Arnold, Randy Kindig, and Kevin Savetz. It has had episodes at least monthly since. There are more than 350 episodes in total. Most of these are interesting interviews with people who worked for Atari or who contributed hardware, software, or other related materials over the years. Some are interesting discussion episodes that feature the hosts and sometimes guests talking about specific topics and news. I have learned tons from *ANTIC*. I recommend starting at the beginning and working your way through. I listened to all the discussion episodes first and am now working my way through many of the interviews. I queue these up on my smartphone and listen to them in the car on my daily commute. A great way to pass the time!

Instructions. You can find these on the *ANTIC* website (https://ataripodcast.libsyn.com) and listen to them on your PC or you can subscribe on your smartphone or mobile device. Most episodes are between 30 minutes and 1.5 hours long. I particularly like the show notes which include links to the sources mentioned in the podcast.

Comments. This podcast is an amazing service to the Atari community. A special thanks to the hosts for all their efforts over the past five plus years. The interviews are important because everyone who worked in the industry back in the 1970s and 1980s is aging and their knowledge of Atari history will eventually disappear. I hope the hosts will be able to keep this going for years to come!

46. Watch the *Fate of Atari* Documentary (2 Hours)

Prerequisites. All you need for this project is a web browser. Expect to spend two hours watching the documentary.

Introduction. The history of Atari is a fascinating story of innovation, business success, and business failure. There must be case studies on Atari which have been developed by business schools across the country. I would love to get my hands on some of those to see what the lessons are and how they are presented. There are several books that go through the history of Atari. I highly recommend the books *Breakout* (see Chapter 41) and *Atari Inc.* (see Chapter 42). I also recommend the documentary *Easy to Learn, Hard to Master: The Fate of Atari* that was directed by Tomaso Walliser and Davide Agosta and was partly funded by a Kickstarter. This history of Atari is well done and features interviews with lots of Atari personnel, including Nolan Bushnell, Al Alcorn, and Joe Decuir. They tell the story of Atari from its inception as the first coin-op video game company with *Computer Space* and *Pong* and later the developer of the Atari 2600. The documentary does not cover the Atari 8-bit or 16-bit home computers or its recent history and ends just before the sale to Jack Tramiel in 1984.

Instructions. Watch *Easy to Learn, Hard to Master: The Fate of Atari*. You can find it online on YouTube, Amazon, iTunes, and others. The price varies but is generally between $2 and $12 to rent or buy.

Comments. I always learn something new when I watch a video or read about the history of Atari. I highly recommend this documentary, although some reviewers think the narration could have been better. I didn't really notice this since much of the content consists of interviews with former Atari personnel.

47. Read the Atari 8-Bit FAQ (15-60 Minutes)

Prerequisites. All you need for this project is a web browser. Expect to spend at least 15 to 60 minutes exploring the FAQ.

Introduction. If you were "online" in the 1980s you probably accessed Usenet newsgroups for posting on discussion threads about various topics, including Atari. There was, and still is, a comp.sys.atari.8bit newsgroup that was quite active in the 1990s. In order to minimize redundancy, many newsgroups came with an FAQ to orient users before they started making posts. The Atari 8-bit newsgroup has an awesome FAQ that was developed and still maintained by Michael Current. This is a great source of information about the Atari 400/800/XL/XE

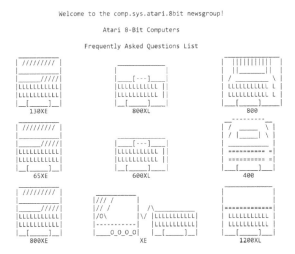

computers and worth at least browsing. There is information about the computers, video display, data storage, printers, modems, software, file formats, and even interfacing with modern computers.

Instructions. Navigate to the FAQ on your browser (https://mcurrent.name/atari-8-bit/faq.txt).

Comments. There is an *ANTIC* podcast (Episode 10) featuring Michael Current. Episode 9 of the *Player/Missile* podcast features an interview with Current. These are helpful for some of the background info about the FAQ.

At the end of the FAQ is an interesting historical timeline of the Atari 8-bit computers.

48. Join Atari Age (5-10 Minutes)

Prerequisites. All you need for this project is a web browser. Expect to spend at least five to 10 minutes registering.

Introduction. As I have rediscovered my love for Atari home computers and video game systems, I have found Atari Age to be a great community of enthusiasts and experts. The Atari Age website (http://atariage.com) is named after the *Atari Age* magazine that was sent to members of the Atari Club from 1982 to 1984.

The website is mostly dedicated to Atari video games for the 2600, 5200, 7800, Lynx, and Jaguar. There is a wealth of information about games for each system, including rarity guides, scans of labels and manuals, FAQs, and hardware. There are also homebrew games and hardware that you can purchase. I particularly like the forums that cover the game systems as well as 8-bit and 16-bit home computers. Relevant here are the forums that cover the Atari 400, 800, XL, and XE series of computers and programming. It is often the case that when I have a coding question, or a question about some specific hardware or software, I can find the answer on Atari Age. Tough questions can be posted here when answers can't be found elsewhere, and one can also respond to posts.

Instructions. Navigate to the Atari Age forums website and create an account. You will need an account to be able to make posts or respond to posts on the forum. You will be asked to provide a handle and to provide a summary of your Atari interests. My handle is scitari and I included a list of my Atari hardware in my profile. Atari Age keeps track of how many times you post and how many people visit your profile.

Comments. For the most part, this is a great community that is ready and willing to help you with your Atari hobby. There are some users who get annoyed if you don't follow protocol or if you ask a question that has already been covered in another post. My advice is to have fun and don't worry about the very few cranky folks.

49. Participate in a Retro Challenge (1 Month)

Prerequisites. For this project, you will need an Atari home computer and whatever other supplies you need for your specific challenge. Expect to spend multiple hours per week over the course of a month.

Introduction. The Retro Challenge started in 2016 as an opportunity for retro-computing enthusiasts and practitioners to enjoy their hobby (http://www.retrochallenge.org). The goal is to start a project with an old computer and then blog about it for a month. That is it! This is open-ended and is really meant to be a motivator to start, and perhaps finish, a project that might otherwise not happen. I have personally not done this yet but would like to. These seem to be held several times a year, in case you miss the next one.

Instructions. Come up with a hardware or software project and then email the host your name, a photo of yourself, your twitter handle, your blog location, and a brief summary of the project you plan to carry out. The idea is that you would send these details before the challenge starts. There are judges and sometimes prizes from what I can tell.

Comments. You can browse past challenges and entries on their website. The projects from April of 2018 ranged from building a replacement joystick for the Atari 5200 to making a new game for the Atari 2600. Many of the projects are hardcore and sound intimidating. However, I think they welcome all projects no matter how sophisticated. Note that many projects are never finished. That is ok. The primary goal is to have fun!

50. Attend a Vintage Computer Festival (1-3 Days)

Prerequisites. For this project, you will need to travel to the location of the Vintage Computer Festival (VCF). Expect to spend one to three days attending the VCF, in addition to travel time.

Introduction. Vintage Computer Festivals (VCF) are annual events held across the United States, and beyond, to educate the public about vintage computers and to celebrate the robust vintage computer community. It is a great opportunity to learn about old systems and to meet like-minded people who share your love for these old machines. Many of the VCFs sprang up organically over the years to meet a local need. Some of these are now managed by the Vintage Computer Federation (http://vcfed.org), which is a non-profit dedicated to supporting hobbyists and to spreading knowledge of computing history.

I attended my first VCF (East) in Wall, NJ in 2019. I was just there for one day and had an awesome time. The day started with a keynote by Ken Thompson, who told several stories about developing UNIX at Bell Labs in the late 1960s and early 1970s. He was joined by Brian Kernighan, who moderated the session. The room was packed as VCF East was celebrating 50 years of UNIX and everyone wanted to meet these two pioneers. The rest of the day consisted of time to visit the vintage computer exhibits, the consignment store, and various workshops on soldering and building single-board computers. I had a great time wandering around, trying different vintage computers, and just taking in the excitement from all the participants.

In addition to celebrating 50 years of UNIX, VCF East was celebrating 40 years of Atari. Joe Decuir gave the keynote (the video is on YouTube) on the last day and the Atari exhibit was the largest seen at any VCF. Allan Bushman, Peter Fletcher, Bill Lange, Curt Vendel (see photo of his exhibit below), and several others were there with beautiful exhibits featuring every Atari 8-bit and 16-bit machine. In addition, Curt brought a number of extremely rare prototypes and short-lived products, such as the 815 disk drive and the 1090 expansion box. These were fun to see in person. I had a wonderful time getting to know the Atari community. In addition to the people mentioned, I also got to meet Nir Dary, Randy Kindig of the *Floppy Days* and *ANTIC* podcasts, and Kevin Savetz of *ANTIC*.

Instructions. Find a VCF near you and go! You will have a great time. Here is a list of the annual VCFs I know about:

VCF East - Wall, NJ
VCF Europe - European countries
VCF Italy - Italy
VCF Midwest - Chicago, IL
VCF Pacific Northwest - Seattle, WA
VCF Southeast - Roswell, GA
VCF West - Mountain View, CA

Comments. Now that I have been to a VCF, I can't wait to go back. If you go, be sure to prepare questions or even bring hardware you are having trouble with. There are many experts there who might be able to help you. It is a good chance to network and get to know the community. It is always more difficult to practice a hobby in isolation. Also, think about doing an exhibit yourself at one of these events. I plan to do one next year.